WEDDING READINGS & MUSICAL IDEAS

Other wedding books from our Wedding Collection

Chapman, Carole, *The Complete Wedding Organiser and Record,*
0-572-02338-3

Chapman, Carole, *Organising your Second Marriage,*0-572-01987-4

Chapman, Carole, *Your Wedding Planner,* 0-572-02415-0

Chapman, Carole and Hobson, Wendy, *Wedding Duties for Men,*
0-572-02761-3

Hobson, Christopher, *The Best Man's Organiser,* 0-572-02303-0

Hobson, Wendy, *The Wedding File,* 0-572-02427-4

Jacqueline Eames, *The Best Best Man,* 0-572-02339-1

Jarvis, Lee, *Wedding Speeches,* 0-572-01781-2

Jeffery, Barbara, *Wedding Speeches and Toasts,* 0-572-02410-X

Mitch Murray's *One-liners for Weddings,* 0-572-01896-7

Pat and Bill Deraugh, *Wedding Etiquette,* 0-572-02409-6

Smith, Helen, *Your Brilliant Wedding Speech,* 0-572-02762-1

Statham, Amanda, *The Modern Bride,* 0-572-02870-9

Available from all good bookshops or telephone Macmillan Direct
on 01256 302699.

WEDDING READINGS & MUSICAL IDEAS

REV. JOHN WYNBURNE
& ALISON GIBBS

foulsham

LONDON • NEW YORK • TORONTO • SYDNEY

foulsham

The Publishing House, Bennetts Close, Cippenham,
Slough, Berkshire, SL1 5AP, England

ISBN 0-572-02861-X

Printed in Great Britain by St Edmundsbury Press Ltd, Bury St Edmunds, Suffolk

Contents

Introduction

A WEDDING IS a very important event: it marks one of
the most significant decisions of your life. As well as having a
serious purpose, it is also a day of celebration, a day of fun and
festivity, a day to cherish and a day that you will want to look
back on again and again.

Organising a wedding is a daunting task. A great deal of
time and money, not to mention hopes and dreams, are usually
invested in the planning, with everyone involved wanting to
enjoy the day to the full and make it a special and
unforgettable experience. The responsibility for the organisers
can, at times, seem overwhelming and it is not always easy to
source the myriad talents and depth of knowledge that are
required. This book is designed to help with two vital aspects
of your wedding: the readings and the music.

Whether it takes place in a sacred building, a register office
or in another licensed location, some elements of a wedding
remain reassuringly constant: the choice of words used for the
vows and the order of events are familiar to most of us.
However, it is possible to add personal touches of style to the
ceremony itself by the use of readings and music that
accompany the event. An appropriate piece of poetry or prose
can often express what we are feeling at a given moment far
more eloquently than we could ourselves and there is no doubt
that music is the perfect way to create the atmosphere you
want. Unfortunately, although most of us can quote a few
verses from the Bible or a phrase from a favourite poem, or
hum a few bars of a familiar piece of music, we may have no
idea of where to find the whole work, what it was called or
who the author or composer was.

This collection is designed to make the task of finding and choosing the readings and music easier for you. We have, in the first sections of the book, brought together a variety of written extracts, both prose and poetry, as well as short readings from the New Revised Standard Version of the Bible. (You can, of course, use a different version if you prefer.) Somewhere in these pages, we hope that you will find a passage that puts into words what you feel most deeply, or helps you and those with you to focus on the meaning and importance of the occasion. Most of the items we have chosen are quite brief – many can be read in less than a minute – and the longer ones may be shortened by cutting out sections if you prefer. The style and language vary from the simplest and most contemporary to the very traditional. Some are humorous, some are thought-provoking, but all are chosen to match in some way the emotions and intentions that surround a marriage.

We have also put together a selection of musical compositions to be performed during the wedding. We have organised them into groups, each designed to establish a mood and enhance the atmosphere at a particular stage of the ceremony. All you have to do is pick out the pieces that you feel match the style of your own individual wedding ceremony.

We hope that, whilst making your choice, you will enjoy reading and listening to the passages and compositions we have suggested and that, once your wedding is over, you will want to keep this book as a reminder of your special, memorable day.

PROSE EXTRACTS

Love Is the River of Life

LOVE IS THE RIVER of life in this world. Think not that ye know it who stand at the little tinkling rill, the first small fountain.

Not until you have gone through the rocky gorges and not lost the stream; not until you have gone through the meadow, and the stream has widened and deepened until fleets could ride on its bosom; not until beyond the meadow you have come to the unfathomable ocean, and poured your treasure into its depths – not until then can you know what love is.

HENRY WARD BEECHER (1813–1887)

Marriage Is a Commitment

MARRIAGE IS A COMMITMENT to take that joy deep, deeper than happiness, deep into the discovery of who you most truly are. It is a commitment to a spiritual journey, to a life of becoming – in which joy can comprehend despair; running through rivers of pain into joy again.

Thus marriage is even deeper than commitment. It is a covenant – a covenant that says: I love you – I trust you – I will be here for you when you are hurting, and when I am hurting I will not leave. It is a covenant intended not to provide a haven from pain or anger or sorrow. Life offers no such haven. Instead, marriage is intended to provide a sanctuary safe enough to risk loving; to risk living and sharing from the centre of oneself.

This is worth everything.

ANONYMOUS

The Voyage of Commitment

THE VOYAGE OF commitment is never made alone; we cannot, then, be committed only to ourselves or we will die. We must ask whether we can give ourselves to another, or to others not knowing the changes that time, bad luck, and sickness may work on them … You have to give more than this in real love, and be ready to move into darkness, illness, and loss of beauty, if you care at all about someone else. We stand on sacred ground when we stand close enough to another to give ourselves without strings, conditions, or codicils written into our commitments. Are such commitments possible? How can we tell unless we have given ourselves to another, made our heart vulnerable, in order to achieve a sense of life which is deeper than the trembling moment and its dreadful ticking uncertainties.

E. KENNEDY

Marriage Is One Long Conversation

MARRIAGE IS ONE long conversation, chequered by disputes. The disputes are valueless; they but ingrain the difference; the heroic heart of woman prompting her at once to nail her colours to the mast. But in the intervals, almost unconsciously, and with no desire to shine, the whole material of life is turned over and over, ideas are struck out and shared, the two persons more and more adapt their notions one to suit the other, and in the process of time, without sound of trumpet, they conduct each other into new worlds of thought.

ROBERT LOUIS STEVENSON (1850–1894)

Marriage Advice

LET YOUR LOVE BE STRONGER than your hate or anger. Learn the wisdom of compromise, for it is better to bend a little that to break. Believe the best rather than the worst. People have a way of living up or down to your opinion of them. Remember that true friendship is the basis for any lasting relationship. The person you choose to marry is deserving of the courtesies and kindnesses you bestow on your friends.

Please hand this down to your children and your children's children.

JANE WELLS (1839–1927)

The Greatest Happiness

YOU CAN GIVE WITHOUT LOVING, but you can never love without giving. The great acts of love are done by those who are habitually performing small acts of kindness. We pardon to the extent that we love. Love is knowing that even when you are alone, you will never be lonely again. And great happiness of life is the conviction that we are loved. Loved for ourselves. And even loved in spite of ourselves.

VICTOR HUGO (1802–1885)
From *Les Misérables*

Marriage Is a Commitment to Life

MARRIAGE IS A COMMITMENT to life, the best that two people can find and bring out in each other. It offers opportunities for sharing and growth that no other relationship can equal. It is a physical and an emotional joining that is promised for a lifetime.

Within the circle of its love, marriage encompasses all of life's most important relationships. A wife and a husband are each other's best friend, confidant, lover, teacher, listener and critic. And there may come times when one partner is heartbroken or ailing, and the love of the other may resemble the tender caring of a parent for a child.

Marriage deepens and enriches every facet of life. Happiness is fuller, memories are fresher, commitment is stronger, even anger is felt more strongly, and passes away more quickly.

Marriage understands and forgives the mistakes life is unable to avoid. It encourages and nurtures new life, new experiences, and new ways of expressing love that is deeper than life.

When two people pledge their love and care for each other in marriage, they create a spirit unique unto themselves which binds them closer than any spoken or written words. Marriage is a promise, a potential made in the hearts of two people who love each other and takes a lifetime to fulfil.

EDMUND O'NEILL (B 1929)

Marriage Is the Beginning of an Enterprise

MARRIAGE IS THE BEGINNING of an enterprise. In theory, two people have decided they love and trust and respect each other well enough to want to spend the rest of their lives together. They will build something that appears to outsiders something infinitely simple, but which in fact, is infinitely complex – an ark to survive all weathers.

In reality, of course, people blunder into marriage for a dozen reasons – and often spend the rest of their lives on a disintegrating raft, held together with pieces of string. But any craft will stay afloat as long as its builders are happier to share its limitations than risk sharks. A boat can be merely a means of survival – or a means to a great discovery. Its course may be erratic, the repairs to its structure constant and haphazard – but if it is still afloat it has, with all its eccentricities, a jaunty air, a lived-in look, an air of comfortable companionship.

PAM BROWN (B 1928)
From *Happy Anniversary*

Never Marry but for Love

NEVER MARRY BUT FOR LOVE; but see that thou lovest what is lovely. He that minds a body and not a soul has not the better part of that relationship, and will consequently lack the noblest comfort of a married life.

Between a man and his wife nothing ought to rule but love. As love ought to bring them together, so it is the best way to keep them well together.

A husband and wife that love one another show their children that they should do so too. Others visibly lose their authority in their families by their contempt of one another, and teach their children to be unnatural by their own examples.

Let not enjoyment lessen, but augment, affection; it being the basest of passions to like when we have not, what we slight when we possess.

Here it is we ought to search out our pleasure, where the field is large and full of variety, and of an enduring nature; sickness, poverty or disgrace being not able to shake it because it is not under the moving influences of worldly contingencies.

Nothing can be more entire and without reserve; nothing more zealous, affectionate and sincere; nothing more contented than such a couple, nor greater temporal felicity than to be one of them.

WILLIAM PENN (1644–1718)

The Mystery of Love

THE MYSTERY OF LOVE is the mystery of personality, which penetrates into another in a unique never-to-be-renewed identity. It is the vision of another's image in God. Only the lover can contemplate the face of the beloved. The image of man is always distorted and obscured for one who does not love. It is only through love that we can see the beauty of the human face. Love is not the confirmation of an identity, the discovery of a single principle in myself and another – *tat twam asi,* as Indian thought would have it. If 'you' and 'I' are but one then my love for you is only the love of myself. There is no longer another being. The loving subject and his love always imply the existence of another and presuppose a going-out of the self towards this other person, the mystery of the union of two beings who enjoy independent and distinct reality.

NIKOLAI ALEXANDROVICH BERDYAEV (1874–1948)

Friendship

IT IS OFTEN SAID that it is love that makes the world go around. However, without doubt, it is friendship which keeps our spinning existence on an even keel.

True friendship provides so many of the essentials for a happy life – it is the foundation on which to build an enduring relationship, it is the mortar which bonds us together in harmony, and it is the calm, warm protection we sometimes need when the world outside seems cold and chaotic.

True friendship holds a mirror to our foibles and failings, without destroying our sense of worthiness. True friendship nurtures our hopes, supports us in our disappointments, and encourages us to grow to our best potential.

[Bride's name] and [groom's name] came together as friends. Today, they pledge to each other not only their love, but also the strength, warmth and, most importantly, the fun of true friendship.

JUDY BIELICKI

A Creed to Live By

DON'T UNDERMINE YOUR WORTH by comparing yourself with others. It is because we are different that each of us is special. Don't set your goals by what other people deem important. Only you know what is best for you. Don't take for granted the things closest to your heart. Cling to them as you would your life, for without them life is meaningless. Don't let your life slip through your fingers by living in the past or for the future. By living your life one day at a time, you live all the days of your life.

Don't give up when you still have something to give. Nothing is really over until the moment you stop trying. Don't be afraid to admit that you are less than perfect. It is this fragile thread that binds us to one another. Don't be afraid to encounter risks. It is by taking chances that we learn how to be brave.

Don't shut love out of your life by saying it's impossible to find. The quickest way to lose love is to hold it too tightly; and the best way to keep love is to give it wings. Don't dismiss your dreams. To be without dreams is to be without hope; to be without hope is to be without purpose. Don't run through life so fast that you forget not only where you've been but also where you're going. Life is not a race, but a journey to be savoured each step of the way.

NANCYE SIMS

Blessing for a Marriage

MAY YOUR MARRIAGE bring you all the exquisite excitements a
marriage should bring, and may life grant you also
patience, tolerance, and understanding.

May you always need one another – not so much to fill your
emptiness as to help you to know your fullness. A
mountain needs a valley to be complete; the valley does not
make the mountain less, but more; and the valley is more a
valley because it has a mountain towering over it. So let it
be with you and you.

May you need one another, but not out of weakness.

May you want one another, but not out of lack.

May you entice one another, but not compel one another.

May you embrace one another, but not out-encircle one
another.

May you succeed in all important ways with one another, and
not fail in the little graces.

May you look for things to praise, often say, 'I love you!' and
take no notice of small faults.

If you have quarrels that push you apart, may both of you
hope to have good sense enough to take the first step back.

May you enter into the mystery which is the awareness of one
another's presence – no more physical than spiritual, warm
and near when you are side by side, and warm and near
when you are in separate rooms or even distant cities.

May you have happiness, and may you find it making one
another happy.

May you have love, and may you find it loving one another!

JAMES DILLET FREEMAN

Married Life

HAVING EMBARKED ON MARRIED LIFE, he saw at every step that it was not at all what he had imagined. At every step he experienced what a man experiences when, after admiring the smooth, happy motion of a boat on a lake, he finds himself sitting in it himself. He found that it was not enough to sit quietly without rocking the boat, that he had constantly to consider what to do next, that not for a moment must he forget what course to steer or that there was water under his feet, that he had to row, much as it hurt his unaccustomed hands, that it was pleasant enough to look at it from the shore, but very hard, though very delightful, to sail it.

LEO TOLSTOY (1828–1910)
From *Anna Karenina*

Happiness

HAPPINESS IS TO BE FOUND among life's common things. It is not great wealth, great learning, great genius or great power; it is not these things that make the possessors happy. It is health, friendship, love at home; it is the voices of children, it is sunshine. It is the blessings that are commonest, not those that are the rarest.

ANONYMOUS

A Father's Words on Love

Dr Iannis is speaking to his daughter Pelagia:

AND ANOTHER THING. Love is a temporary madness, it erupts like volcanoes and then subsides. And when it subsides you have to make a decision. You have to work out whether your roots have so entwined together that it is inconceivable that you should ever part. Because this is what love is. Love is not breathlessness, it is not excitement, it is not the promulgation of promises of eternal passion … it is not lying awake imagining he is kissing every cranny of your body. No, don't blush, I am telling you some truths. That is just being 'in love', which any fool can do. Love itself is what is left over when being in love has burned away, and this is both an art and a fortunate accident. Your mother and I had it, we had roots that grew towards each other underground, and when all the pretty blossom had fallen from our branches, we found that we were one tree and not two.

LOUIS DE BERNIÈRES
From *Captain Corelli's Mandolin*

On Love

THE LOVE OF GOD, unutterable and perfect,
flows into a pure soul the way that light
rushes into a transparent object.
The more love that it finds, the more it gives itself,
so that, as we grow more clear and open,
the more complete the joy of loving is.
And the more souls who resonate together,
the greater the intensity of their love,
for, mirror-like, each soul reflects the others.

> DANTE (1265–1321)
> From *The Divine Comedy*

The Most Wonderful of All Things

THE MOST WONDERFUL OF ALL THINGS in life is the discovery of
another human being with whom one's relationship has
growing depth, beauty and joy as the years increase. This
inner progressiveness of love between two human beings is a
most marvelous thing; it cannot be found by looking for it or
by passionately wishing for it. It is a sort of divine accident,
and the most wonderful of all things in life.

> SIR HUGH WALPOLE (1884–1941)

Marriage Is a Dynamic Process

MARRIAGE is a dynamic process of discovery.

Marriage is a journey, not an arrival.

In marriage, being the right person is as important as finding the right person.

Marriage is starting to love, over and over again.

Marriage is a life's work.

Marriage is an art ... and like any creative process, it requires active thought and effort.

We have to learn how to share on many different levels.

We need to practise talking from the heart, and understanding attitudes as well as words.

Giving generously and receiving graciously are talents that are available to anyone.

But all these skills need to be developed, if the marriage picture that we paint is to be anything approaching the masterpiece intended.

ANONYMOUS

On Love and Relationships

WHEN YOU LOVE SOMEONE, you do not love them all the time, in exactly the same way, from moment to moment. It is an impossibility. It is even a lie to pretend to. And yet this is exactly what most of us demand. We have so little faith in the ebb and flow of life, of love, of relationships. We leap at the flow of the tide and resist in terror its ebb. We are afraid it will never return. We insist on permanency, on duration, on continuity; when the only continuity possible, in life as in love, is in growth, in fluidity – in freedom, in the sense that the dancers are free, barely touching as they pass, but partners in the same pattern.

The only real security is not in owning or possessing, not in demanding or expecting, not in hoping, even. Security in a relationship lies neither in looking back to what was in nostalgia, nor forward to what it might be in dread or anticipation, but living in the present relationship and accepting it as it is now. Relationships must be like islands, one must accept them for what they are here and now, within their limits – islands, surrounded and interrupted by the sea, and continually visited and abandoned by the tides ...

It takes years to marry completely two hearts, even of the most loving and well assorted. A happy wedlock is a long falling in love. Young persons think love belongs only to the brown-haired and crimson-cheeked. So it does for its beginning. But the golden marriage is a part of love which the Bridal day knows nothing of ...

Such a large and sweet fruit is a complete marriage that it needs a long summer to ripen, and then a long winter to mellow and season it. But a really happy marriage of love and judgment between a noble man and woman is one of the things so very handsome that if the sun were, as the Greek poets fabled, a God, he might stop the world and hold it still now and then in order to look all day long on some example thereof, and feast his eyes on such a spectacle.

ANNE MORROW LINDBERGH (1906–2001)
From *Gift from the Sea*

The Demands of Love

FOR ONE HUMAN BEING to love another: that is perhaps the most difficult of all tasks, the ultimate task, the final test and proof, the work for which all other work is but preparation.

Love is at first not anything that means merging, surrendering, and uniting with another (for what purpose would a union of something unclarified serve?), rather it is a high inducement to the individual to ripen, to become something in ourselves, to become a world in ourselves for the sake of another person. Love is a great demanding claim on us, something that chooses us and calls us to vast distances.

RAINER MARIA RILKE (1875–1926)
From *Letters to a Young Poet*

Love Is

LOVE IS; and makes all the rules itself, according to the multiple needs of the lover. We can all of us imagine what love should be, love being one of our earliest unshakeable certainties – having nourished it since childhood as a symbol of private magic, transfixed with our special demands and wishes. Our image of love is the spell we put on others – or fancy we do at least – in order to compel them to enter that particular part of ourselves which egoism has hollowed out to receive them. Indefatigable love-seekers all, spending the bulk of our energies to this end, why then are we so often defeated, finding durable love more difficult to win than almost any other ambition?

To be in love, of course, is to take on the pent-house of living, that topmost toppling tower, perpetually lit by the privileged radiance of well-being which sets one apart from the nether world. Born, we are mortal, dehydrated, ordinary; love is the oil that plumps one up, dilates the eyes, puts a glow on the skin, lifts us free from the weight of time, and helps us see in some other that particular kind of beauty which is the crown of our narcissism.

Love also brings into our lives that mysterious apparition called style, the special fluency of our acts and feelings, so that we are dressed, while it lasts, in the flashy garments of supermen, omnipotent, supercharged. Love is also disquiet, the brooding pleasures of doubt, midnights wasted by speculation, the frantic dance round the significance of the last thing she said, the need to see her to have life confirmed. At best, love is simply the slipping of a hand in another's, of knowing you are where you belong at last, and of exchanging through the eyes that all-consuming regard which ignores everybody else on earth.

Laurie Lee (1914–1997)
From *I Can't Stay Long*

The Depth of Love

REAL LOVE IS an all-consuming, desperate yearning for the beloved, who is perceived as different, mysterious, and elusive. The depth of love is measured by the intensity of obsession with the loved one. There is little time or attention for other interests or pursuits, because so much energy is focused on recalling past encounters or imagining future ones. Often, great obstacles must be overcome, and thus there is an element of suffering in true love. Another indication of the depth of love is the willingness to endure pain and hardship for the sake of the relationship. Associated with real love are feelings of excitement, rapture, drama, anxiety, tension, mystery, and yearning.

Real love is a partnership to which two caring people are deeply committed. These people share many basic values, interests and goals, and tolerate good-naturedly their individual differences. The depth of love is measured by the mutual trust and respect they feel toward each other. Their relationship allows each to be more fully expressive, creative, and productive in the world. There is much joy in shared experiences both past and present, as well as those that are anticipated. Each views the other as his/her dearest and most cherished friend. Another measure of the depth of love is the willingness to look honestly at oneself in order to promote the growth of the relationship and the deepening of intimacy. Associated with real love are feelings of serenity, devotion, understanding, companionship, mutual support, and comfort.

ROBIN NORWOOD
From *Women Who Love Too Much*

Hand of the Bride and Groom

[BRIDE'S NAME], please face [*groom's name*], and hold his hands, palms up, so you may see the gift that they are to you. These are the hands that will passionately love you and cherish you through the years, for a lifetime of happiness. These are the hands that will countless times wipe the tears from your eyes: tears of sorrow and tears of joy. These are the hands that will comfort you in illness, and hold you when fear or grief fill you. These are the hands that will give you support and celebrate with you in your accomplishments.

[*Groom's name*], please hold [*bride's name*]'s hands, palms up, where you may see the gift that they are to you. These are the hands that will hold you tight as you struggle through difficult times. They are the hands that will comfort you when you are sick or console you when you are grieving. These are the hands that will passionately love you and cherish you through the years, for a lifetime of happiness. These are the hands that will give you support as she encourages you to fulfil your dreams. Together, as a team, everything you wish for can be realized.

ANONYMOUS

Marriage Is the Greatest Happiness of All

IN A MARRIAGE, two people become as one, yet they are individuals, each with their own ideas and goals. In a marriage, two people share their thoughts, they give advice, sharing their feelings, being open and loving. They must trust each other and hold onto faith, while going through ups and downs. They have their smiles, and they have their tears. When one is low, it is up to the other to support them, to get them back on the right track. Communication is the key.

Two people united learn so much. They learn to depend yet to be independent, sometimes letting each other have time to themselves. They care for each other and protect; they make a family and become a lifeline. They begin their dreams, their future, loving and growing together. With their commitment and true love, they find happiness.

MICHELE GALLAGHER (B 1943)

The Sanctity of Marriage

GOD IS GUIDING YOUR MARRIAGE. Marriage is more than your love for each other. It has a higher dignity and power. For it is God's holy ordinance, by means of which He wills to perpetuate the human race until the end of time. In your love you see your two selves as solitary figures in the world; in marriage you see yourselves as links in the chain of the generations which God causes to come and go to His glory and calls into His Kingdom. In your love you see only the heaven of your bliss, through marriage you are placed at a post of responsibility towards the world and towards mankind. Your love is your own private possession; marriage is more than a private affair, it is an estate, an office. As the crown makes the King, and not just his determination to rule, so marriage and not just your love for each other makes you husband and wife in the sight of God and man. As you first gave the ring to one another and received it a second time from the hand of the parson, so love comes from you, but marriage from above, from God. As God is infinitely higher than man, so the sanctity, the privilege and the promise of marriage are higher than the sanctity, the privilege and the promise of love. It is not your love which sustains the marriage, but from now on the marriage which sustains your love.

DEITRICH BONHOEFFER (1906–1945)
From *Letters and Papers from Prison*

Views on Marriage

WHAT GREATER THING is there for two human souls than to feel that they are joined for life – to strengthen each other in all labour, to rest on each other in all sorrow, to minister to each other in all pain, to be one with each other in silent, unspeakable memories at the moment of the last parting.

GEORGE ELIOT (1819–1880)

MARRIAGE HAS IN IT less of beauty, but more of safety, than the single life; it hath not more ease; but less danger; it is more merry and more sad; it is fuller of sorrows and fuller of joys; it lies under more burdens, but is supported by all the strengths of love and charity; and those burdens are delightful. Marriage is the mother of the world, and preserves kingdoms, and fills cities ...

JEREMY TAYLOR (1613–1667)

KINDNESS IS THE LIFE'S BLOOD, the elixir of marriage. Kindness makes the difference between passion and caring. Kindness is tenderness. Kindness is love, but perhaps greater than love ... Kindness is good will. Kindness says, 'I want you to be happy'.

RANDOLPH RAY
From *My Little Church around the Corner*

TWO PERSONS who have chosen each other out of all the species, with the design to be each other's mutual comfort and entertainment, have, in that action, bound themselves to be good-humoured, affable, discreet, forgiving, patient, and joyful, with respect to each other's frailties and perfections, to the end of their lives.

JOSEPH ADDISON (1672–1719)

CHAINS DO NOT HOLD a marriage together. It is threads, hundreds of tiny threads which sew people together through the years. That is what makes a marriage last.

SIMONE SIGNORET (1921–1985)

MARRIAGE LENDS PERMANENCE and a public shape to Love. Marriage vows are made by a man and woman to one another, but they are also made before the world, which is formally present at the ceremony in the role of witness. Marriage solemnizes love, giving this most inward of feelings an outward form ...

JOHNATHAN SCHNELL
From *The Fate of the Earth*

Peace and Love

PEACE DOES NOT COME through the agreement of egos, for it is impossible for egos to agree. Peace comes when love and mutual respect are present. When love is present, your enemy becomes like a friend who is not afraid to disagree with you. You do not cast him out of your heart just because he sees things differently from you. You listen carefully to what he has to say.

When you listen to your enemy the same way that you would listen to your friend, it is not your ego doing the listening. The Spirit inside of you is listening to the Spirit inside of him.

The cause of all human conflict is a simple one: each side dehumanises the other. Each side sees the other as less worthy. As long as each side perceives the other this way, even the simplest details cannot be negotiated. But let each side bring to the other the attitude of respect and acceptance, and even difficult details will be resolved.

Miracles come from love. The solutions that come from loving minds are without limit. The willingness to love – to regard each other as equals – is the essence behind all miracle making.

PAUL FERRINI
From *Love without Conditions*

Learning to Love

ONE MUST LEARN TO LOVE, and go through a good deal of suffering to get to it, like any knight of the grail, and the journey is always towards the other soul, not away from it. Do you think love is an accomplished thing, the day it is recognized? It isn't. To love, you have to learn to understand the other, more than she understands herself, and to submit to her understanding of you. It is damnably difficult and painful, but it is the only thing which endures. You mustn't think that your desire or your fundamental need is to make a good career, or to fill your life with activity, or even to provide for your family materially. It isn't. Your most vital necessity in this life is that you shall love your wife completely and implicitly and in entire nakedness of body and spirit. Then you will have peace and inner security, no matter how many things go wrong.

D.H. LAWRENCE (1885–1930)
From *Selected Letters*

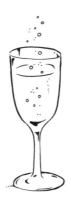

Intimacy and Fidelity in Marriage

THE MOVEMENT INTO MARRIAGE involves the risks of intimacy. In marriage I must be able to come close to you in a way that lets you know and influence me. I must face the risk of being changed, of coming to a different awareness of who I am as a result of our life together. I must accept the responsibility of my own influence in your life as well. Intimacy involves an overlapping of space, a willingness to be influenced, and openness to the possibility of change. It invites me beyond myself ...

Fidelity is the virtue at the core of the lifelong commitment of marriage. In the phrase 'lifelong commitment' we begin to glimpse the complexity of this virtue: commitment suggests stability and lifelong implies change ... Marital fidelity combines commitment and change as two persons seek to grow in the same direction; fidelity is the careful tending of both the commitments and the changes necessary in a maturing love.

EVELYN AND JAMES WHITEHEAD
From *Marrying Well*

Love and Being in Love

BEING IN LOVE IS A GOOD THING, but it is not the best thing. There are many things below it, but there are also things above it. You cannot make it the basis of a whole life. It is a noble feeling, but it is still a feeling ... who could bear to live in that excitement for even five years? ... But, of course, ceasing to be 'in love' need not mean ceasing to love. Love in a second sense – love as distinct from 'being in love' – is not merely a feeling. It is a deep unity, maintained by will and deliberately strengthened by habit; reinforced by (in Christian marriages) the grace which both parents ask, and receive, from God. They can have this love for each other even at those moments when they do not like each other; as you love yourself even when you do not like yourself. They can retain this love even when each would easily, if they allowed themselves, be 'in love' with someone else. 'Being in love' first moved them to promise fidelity: this quieter love enables them to keep the promise. It is on this love that the engine of marriage is run; being in love was the explosion that started it.

C.S. LEWIS (1898–1963)
From *Mere Christianity*

The Path of Marriage

THE MEANING OF MARRIAGE begins in the giving of words. We cannot join ourselves to one another without giving, for in joining ourselves to one another we join ourselves to the unknown. We can join one another only by joining the unknown. We must not be misled by the procedures of experimental thought: in life, in the world, we are never given two known results to choose between, but only one result: that we choose without knowing what it is ...

Because the condition of marriage is worldly and its meaning communal, no one party to it can be solely in charge. What you alone think it ought to be, it is not going to be. Where you alone think you want it to go, it is not going to go. It is going where the two of you – and marriage, time, history and the world – will take it. You do not know the road; you have committed your life to a way.

WENDELL BERRY (B 1934)
From *Standing by Words*

A Marriage Prayer

As we begin our journey down the road of life together. We
don't know what lies ahead for the road turns and bends.
But help us to make the best of whatever comes our way.

Help us to hug each other often ... laugh a lot, talk more, and
argue less.

Help us to continue to enjoy each other as we did when we
first met.

Help us to realize that nothing or no one is perfect and to look
for the good in all things and all people including ourselves.

Help us to respect each other's likes and dislikes, opinions and
beliefs, hopes and dreams and fears even though we may
not always understand them.

Help us to learn from each other and to help each other to
grow mentally, emotionally, and spiritually.

Help us to realize that there is design and purpose in our lives
as in the world and no matter what happens to us we will
hold on to each other and know that things have a way of
working out for the good.

Help us to create for our children a peaceful, stable home of
love as a foundation on which they can build their lives.

But most of all, help us to keep lit the torch of love that we
now share in our hearts so that by our loving example we
may pass on the light of love to our children and to their
children and to their children's children forever.

Bud Henry Bowen

Freedom within Marriage

IF WE COMMIT OURSELVES to one person for life this is not, as many people think, a rejection of freedom; rather, it demands the courage to move into all the risks of freedom, and the risk of love which is permanent; into that love which is not possession but participation ... When love is not possession, but participation, then it is part of that co-creation which is our human calling ... If our love for each other really is participatory, then all other human relationships nourish it; it is inclusive, never exclusive.

MADELEINE L'ENGLE (B 1918)
From *The Crosswick Diaries*

We're Too Old to Be Single

WE'RE TOO OLD TO BE SINGLE. Why shouldn't we both be married instead of sitting through the long winter evenings by our solitary firesides? Why shouldn't we make one fireside of it?

Come, let's be a comfortable couple and take care of each other! How glad we shall be, that we have somebody we are fond of always, to talk to and sit with.

Let's be a comfortable couple. Now do, my dear!

CHARLES DICKENS (1812–1870)
From *Nicholas Nickleby*

Love is Eternal

ROMANTIC LOVE IS ETERNALLY ALIVE; as the self's most urgent
quest, as grail of our hopes of happiness, as the untarnished
source of the tragic, the exalted, the extreme and the beautiful
in modern life. The late twentieth century is the first to open
itself up to the promise of love as the focus of universal
aspirations ...

In the marriage ceremony, that moment when falling in
love is replaced by the arduous drama of staying in love, the
words 'in sickness and in health, for richer, for poorer, till
death do us part' set love in the temporal context in which it
achieves its meaning. As time begins to elapse, one begins to
love the other because they have shared the same experience ...
Selves may not intertwine; but lives do, and shared memory
becomes as much a bond as the bond of the flesh ...

Family love is this dynastic awareness of time, this shared
belonging to a chain of generations ... we collaborate together
to root each other in a dimension of time longer than our own
lives.

MICHAEL IGNATIEFF (B 1947)
From *Lodged in the Heart and Memory*

The Language of Love

AT THAT MOMENT, it seemed to him that time stood still, and
the Soul of the World surged within him. When he looked
into her dark eyes, and saw that her lips were poised between
a laugh and silence, he learned the most important part of the
language that all the world spoke – the language that
everyone on earth was capable of understanding in their heart.
It was love. Something older than humanity, more ancient
than the desert. Something that exerted the same force
whenever two pairs of eyes met, as had theirs here at the well.
She smiled, and that was certainly an omen – the omen he had
been awaiting, without even knowing he was, for all his life.
The omen he had sought to find with his sheep and in his
books, in the crystals and in the silence of the desert.

It was the pure Language of the World. It required no
explanation, just as the universe needs none as it travels
through endless time. What the boy felt at that moment was
that he was in the presence of the only woman in his life, and
that with no need for words, she recognized the same thing.
He was more certain of it than of anything in the world. He
had been told by his parents and grandparents that he must fall
in love and really know a person before becoming committed.
But maybe people who felt that way had never learned the
universal language. Because, when you know that language, it's
easy to understand that someone in the world awaits you,
whether it's in the middle of the desert or in some great city.

And when two such people encounter each other, and their eyes meet, the past and the future become unimportant. There is only that moment, and the incredible certainty that everything under the sun has been written by one hand only. It is the hand that evokes love, and creates a twin soul for every person in the world. Without such love, one's dreams would have no meaning.

PAULO COELHO
From *The Alchemist*

I Hereby Give Myself

I HEREBY GIVE MYSELF. I love you. You are the only being whom I can love absolutely with my complete self, with all my flesh and mind and heart. You are my mate, my perfect partner, and I am yours. You must feel this now, as I do … It was a marvel that we ever met. It is some kind of divine luck that we are together now. We must never, never part again. We are, here in this, necessary beings like gods. As we look at each other we verify, we know the perfection of our love, we recognize each other. Here is my life, here if need be is my death.

IRIS MURDOCH (1919–1999)
From *The Book and the Brotherhood*

Limitless Love

LOVE FLIES, runs and rejoices; it is free and nothing can hold it back. It gives all for all, and has all in all, because it rests in the highest good, from whom all goodness originates and flows. It doesn't look to the gifts, but to the giver of all good things. Love often knows no limits, but burns beyond every limit. Love feels no burden, shrinks from no effort, aims beyond its strength, sees nothing as impossible, for it believes that all things are possible and allowable to it. Thus it is capable of everything, and it succeeds because it is confident of the result, while someone without love loses courage and gives up.

Love keeps watch and is never unaware, even when it sleeps; tired, it is never exhausted; hindered, it is never defeated; alarmed, it is never afraid; but like a living flame and a burning torch it bursts upward and blazes forth.

Love is quick, sincere, dutiful, joyous, and pleasant; brave, patient, faithful, prudent, serene, and vigorous; and it never seeks itself. For whenever we seek ourselves, we fall away from love. Love is watchful, humble, and upright; not weak, or frivolous, or directed toward vain things; temperate, pure, steady, calm, and alert in all the senses. Love is devoted and thankful to God, always trusting and hoping in him, even when it doesn't taste his sweetness, for without pain no one can live in love.

THOMAS À KEMPIS (1379–1471)
From *The Imitation of Christ*

Active Love

ACTIVE LOVE is a harsh and fearful thing compared with love in dreams. Love in dreams thirsts for immediate action, quickly performed, and with everyone watching. Indeed, it will go as far as the giving of one's life, provided it does not take long but is soon over, as on stage, and everyone is looking on and praising. Whereas active love is labour and perseverance, and for some people, perhaps, a whole science. But I predict that even in that very moment when you see with horror that despite all your efforts, you not only have not come nearer your goal but seem to have become farther from it, at that very moment – I predict this to you – you will suddenly reach your goal and will clearly behold over you the wonder-working power of the Lord, who all the while has been loving you and all the while has been mysteriously guiding you.

FYODOR DOSTOEVSKY (1821–1881)
From *The Brothers Karamazov*

The Effects of Marriage

A MARRIAGE ... makes of two fractional lives a whole; it gives to two purposeless lives a work, and doubles the strength of each to perform it; it gives to two questioning natures a reason for living, and something to live for; it will give a new gladness to the sunshine, a new fragrance to the flowers, a new beauty to the earth, and a new mystery to life.

MARK TWAIN (1835–1910)

Pastoral Introduction to the Marriage Service

A WEDDING IS ONE OF LIFE'S GREAT MOMENTS, a time of solemn commitment as well as good wishes, feasting and joy. St John tells us how Jesus shared in such an occasion at Cana, and gave there a sign of new beginnings as he turned water into wine.

Marriage is intended by God to be a creative relationship, as his blessing enables husband and wife to love and support each other in good times and in bad, and to share in the care and upbringing of all children. For Christians, marriage is also an invitation to share life together in the spirit of Jesus Christ. It is based upon a solemn, public and life-long covenant between a man and a woman, declared and celebrated in the presence of God and before witnesses.

On this their wedding day the bride and bridegroom face each other, make their promises and receive God's blessing. You are witnesses of the marriage, and express your support by your presence and your prayers. Your support does not end today: the couple will value continued encouragement in the days and years ahead of them.

Love is patient; love is kind; love is not envious or boastful or arrogant or rude. It does not insist on its own way; it is not irritable or resentful; it does not rejoice in wrongdoing, but rejoices in the truth. It bears all things, believes all things, hopes all things, endures all things. (I CORINTHIANS 13: 4–7)

From *Common Worship: Pastoral Services*
Church of England

The Pledge of Love

HE WENT ON WITH THAT FANTASY, but at this point Kate ceased
to attend. He saw after a little that she had been following
some thought of her own, and he had been feeling the growth
of something determinant even through the extravagance of
much of the pleasantry, the warm transparent irony, into
which their livelier intimacy kept plunging like a confident
swimmer. Suddenly she said to him with extraordinary
beauty: 'I engage myself to you for ever.'

The beauty was in everything, and he could have separated
nothing – couldn't have thought of her face as distinct from the
whole joy. Yet her face had a new light. 'And I pledge you – I
call God to witness! – every spark of my faith; I give you every
drop of my life.' That was all, for the moment, but it was
enough, and it was almost as quiet as if it were nothing. They
were in the open air, in an alley of the Gardens; the great space,
which seemed to arch just then higher and spread wider for
them, threw them back into deep concentration. They moved
by a common instinct to a spot, within sight, that struck them
as fairly sequestered, and there, before their time together was
spent, they had exorted from concentration every advance it
could make them. They had exchanged vows and tokens,
sealed their rich compact, solemnized, so far as breathed words
and murmured sounds and lighted eyes and clasped hands
could do it, their agreement to belong only, and to belong
tremendously, to each other.

HENRY JAMES (1843–1916)
From *The Wings of a Dove*

On Holy Matrimony

THE GOD OF HEAVEN so join you now, as that you may be glad of one another all your life; and when He who hath joined you shall separate you again, establish you with an assurance that He hath but borrowed one of you for a time, to make both your joys the more perfect in the Resurrection.

THE GOD OF HEAVEN make you always of one will, and that will always conformable to His; conserve you in the sincere truth of His religion; feast you with the best feast – [the] peace of conscience; and carry you through the good opinion and love of His saints in this world to the association of His saints and angels, and one another, in the resurrection, and [the] everlasting possession of that kingdom, which His Son, our Saviour Christ Jesus, hath purchased for us with the inestimable price of His incorruptible blood.

JOHN DONNE (1571–1631)
From a sermon preached in 1627

I Promise

I PROMISE to give you the best of myself
  and to ask of you no more than you can give.
I promise to respect you as your own person
  and to realise that your interests, desires and needs
  are no less important than my own.
I promise to share with you my time and my attention
  and to bring joy, strength and imagination to our relationship.
I promise to keep myself open to you,
  to let you see through the window of my world into my
  innermost fears and feelings, secrets and dreams.
I promise to grow along with you,
  to be willing to face changes in order to keep our
  relationship alive and exciting.
I promise to love you in good times and in bad,
  with all I have to give and all I feel inside in the only way
  I know how.

Completely and forever.

DOROTHY R. COLGAN

Litany for a Wedding

WE TAKE DELIGHT in our very presence here in soundness of
body and mind: for our ability to make decisions and the
energy to carry them out.

We remember in this precious moment all those in pain and
who suffer strictures in mind or debilitation of limb. For
what we have, what we are and what we may become – we
are thankful.

We celebrate our common life with friends and family and all
the relationships that sustain our humour and support our
spirits especially in time of trouble or sadness.

We remember in this timeless moment the lonely and the
unloved and those who belong to none, are answerable to
none and upon whom none depend. For what we have,
what we are and what we may become – we are thankful.

We cherish our work, our responsibilities and the where-with-
all that sustains our life-styles: for demands made upon us
which bring out the best and opportunities that enliven our
imaginations.

We remember in this moment of enchantment the unloved
and the purposeless and those whose talents lie
undiscovered or remain wasted. For what we have, what
we are and what we may become – we are thankful.

We delight on this special day in the security of our families
and the protection of reliable affections: in those spaces
wherein love and knowledge may mature especially for
these two friends – [bride's name] and [groom's name].

We remember in this moment those without homes and
without hope; those who, despite their efforts, have come
by so little and who know anxiety too well. For what we
have, what we are and what we may become – we are
thankful.

We are privileged to be here in these profound moments
beyond ordinary time with these two folk: may their vows
rekindle our own and their life together be both a
celebration and a yes to all that abides deeply and remains
constant: faith, hope and that most robust and forgiving of
affections: love.

Anonymous

Love's Hidden Treasure

SOONER OR LATER we begin to understand that love is more
than verses on valentines, and romance in the movies. We
begin to know that love is here and now, real and true, the
most important thing in our lives. For love is the creator of our
favourite memories and the foundation of our fondest dreams.

Love is a promise that is always kept, a fortune that can
never be spent, a seed that can flourish in even the most
unlikely of places. And this radiance that never fades, this
mysterious and magical joy, is the greatest treasure of all – one
known only by those who love.

Anonymous

The Change Brought by Commitment

UNTIL ONE IS COMMITTED there is hesitancy, the chance to draw back, always ineffectiveness. Concerning all acts of initiative and creation, there is one elementary truth, the ignorance of which kills countless ideas and splendid plans: that the moment one definitely commits oneself, then Providence moves too.

All sorts of things occur to help one that would never otherwise have occurred. A whole stream of events issues from the decision, raising in one's favour all manner of unforeseen incidents and meetings and material assistance which no one could have dreamt would have come one's way.

I have learned a deep respect for Goethe's couplet:

Whatever you can do, or dream you can, begin it!
Boldness has genius, power and magic in it!

W.H. MURRAY

The Roots of Marriage

'GO DEEPER THAN LOVE,' D.H. Lawrence wrote, 'for the soul
has greater depths.' The willingness to go deeper than love
itself is a kind of love, a desire to meet the beloved beyond
desire, in the darkness where there is no self, no other. For this
meeting, a man and a woman must be whole enough in
themselves to step out of themselves, into a place of mutual
transformation. They are able to surrender everything they
know, everything they love, with the abandon that a Master
has at the hour of death. Transformation is a death. It is also a
birth, and can be as painful as any physical birth. Painful or
ecstatic, it requires a fundamental trust. 'Into your hands I
commit my spirit.'

A man and a woman who enter this depth of intimacy find
themselves standing in the garden where Adam and Eve stood.
All things are possible for them. The ancient Chinese sage
Tzu-ssu said, 'For the mature person, the Tao begins in the
relation between man and woman, and ends in the infinite
vastness of the universe.' They have traced their love for each
other back to the root of love, the radiant non-self, the
boddhisattva's serene compassion. Like the wedding ring, it has
no beginning, no end.

STEPHEN MITCHELL
From *The Tao of Marriage*

What Is Love?

LOVE IS not just looking at each other and saying 'You're
    wonderful'.
There are times when we are anything but wonderful.
Love is looking out in the same direction. It is linking our
    strength to pull a common load. It is pushing together
    towards the far horizons, hand in hand.
Love is knowing that when our strength falters, we can
    borrow the strength of someone who cares. Love is a
    strange awareness that out sorrows will be shared and
    made lighter by sharing; that joys will be enriched and
    multiplied by the joy of another.
Love is knowing someone else cares that we are not alone
    in life.

ANONYMOUS

POETRY

Deep in My Heart

Deep in my heart, my love will flower,
it is for you I long, love.
You fill my every waking hour,
you are my evening song, love.

I wish you all that's good and gold,
and pleasures ever-new, love;
but best by far, to have and hold,
my heart's desire is you, love.

My food and drink, my life indeed,
until my dying day, love;
my only joy, my every need,
come be my own, O stay, love.

MICHAEL FORSTER
Based on the German of Peter Cornelius

Untitled

A portion of your soul has been entwined with mine.
A gentle kind of togetherness, while separate we stand.
As two trees deeply rooted in separate plots of ground,
while their topmost branches come together,
forming a miracle of lace against the heavens.

ANONYMOUS

I Wanna Be Yours

I wanna be your vacuum cleaner
Breathing in your dust,
I wanna be your Ford Cortina
I will never rust,
If you like your coffee hot
Let me be your coffee pot,
You call the shots,
I wanna be yours.
I wanna be your raincoat
For those frequent rainy days,
I wanna be your dreamboat
When you want to sail away,
Let me be your teddy bear
Take me with you anywhere,
I don't care,
I wanna be yours.
I wanna be your electric meter
I will not run out,
I wanna be the electric heater
You'll get cold without,
I wanna be your setting lotion
Hold your hair in deep devotion,
Deep as the deep Atlantic ocean
That's how deep is my devotion.

JOHN COOPER CLARKE (B 1949)

Only God Knows

Only God knows how wide and deep the love in my heart
    flows
only He understands where I've been and where I now go
I've come to realize that no one here on this earth can
    comprehend
the life experiences I've gone through from beginning to end

It's hard for me to really feel love, real love, heaven sent love
but I feel that for you, my love, it's true my love, it's from
    above
Because I could never create this kind of feeling on my very
    own
what I feel blooms from a passion whose seeds were sewn long
    ago

You can choose to believe me, my love, or hide in the safety of
    your routine
I would not blame you, if you fled in fear, but I would still
    love you, just the same
See you can never completely run from something that God
    meant to be
and once you open your heart, love, and find your faith, you'll
    be able to see

I gave up hiding in fear and pretending to be something that
  I'm not
and I lost several close relationships because I'm not fulfilling
  what these folks want
but at last I'm free, free to be me, free to understand God's
  will for my heart
and I'm telling you I love you, unabashedly, and it would be a
  sin if we were to part

LAMPLIGHTERSPEN

Love Is Life's End

Love is life's end (an end, but never ending)
All joys, all sweets, all happiness awarding;
Love is life's wealth
(ne'er spent, but ever spending),
More rich by giving, taking by discarding;
Love's life's reward, rewarded in rewarding;
Then from thy wretched heart
Fond care remove;
Ah, should thou live but once
Love's sweets to prove.
Thou wilt not love to live unless
Thou live to love.

ANONYMOUS

Now Touch the Air Softly

Now touch the air softly, step gently, one, two ...
I'll love you 'til roses are robin's egg blue;
I'll love you 'til gravel is eaten for bread,
And lemons are orange, and lavender's red.

Now touch the air softly, swing gently the broom.
I'll love you 'til windows are all of a room;
And the table is laid, and the table is bare,
And the ceiling reposes on bottomless air.

I'll love you 'til heaven rips the stars from his coat,
And the moon rows away in a glass-bottomed boat;
And Orion steps down like a river below,
And earth is ablaze, and oceans aglow.

So touch the air softly, and swing the broom high.
We will dust the grey mountains, and sweep the blue sky:
And I'll love you as long as the furrow the plough,
As however is ever, and ever is now.

WILLIAM JAY SMITH (B 1918)
From *A Pavane for the Nursery*

Come Walk with Me

Come walk with me, my love,
Along the paths of life.
And keep up by my side, my love,
As we walk the paths of life.

Stop for a while with me, my love,
The path is growing steep.
We'll sit by the pool of life, my love,
Where the waters are so deep.

We'll follow the stream of life from whence it flows
And seek its very source.
Follow the stream of life, my love,
We'll follow the stream of life.

Come climb these rocks with me, my love,
And help me along the way.
And together we'll reach the top, my love,
We'll stand at the very top.

Look down on the world with me, my love,
Look down on this world of ours.
We walked through life together, my love,
Together we passed the hours.

And we'll continue walking onwards
Through life's more peaceful paths.

JUDITH CALVER

On Friendship

I love you, not for what you are, but what I am, when I am
   with you.
I love you not only for what you have made of yourself, but
   what you are making of me.
I love you for the part of me that you bring out.

I love you for putting your hand into my heaped-up heart and
   passing over all the frivolous and weak things that you
   cannot help seeing there, and drawing out into the light all
   the beautiful and radiant things that no one else has looked
   quite far enough to find.

I love you for ignoring the possibilities of the fool in me, and
   for laying hold of the possibilities of good in me.

I love you for closing your eyes to the discords in me, and
   adding to the music in me by worshipful listening ...

You have done it without a touch, without a sign. You have
   done it by being yourself.

ROY CROFT

On Your Wedding Day

Today is a day you will always remember
    The greatest in anyone's life
You'll start off the day just two people in love
    And end it as Husband and Wife.
It's a brand new beginning, the start of a journey
    With moments to cherish and treasure
And although there'll be times when you both disagree
    These will surely be outweighed by pleasure.
You'll have heard many words of advice in the past
    When the secrets of marriage were spoken
But you know that the answers lie hidden inside
    Where the bond of true love lies unbroken.
So live happy forever as lovers and friends
    It's the dawn of a new life for you
As you stand there together with love in your eyes
    From the moment you whisper 'I do'.
And with luck, all your hopes, and your dreams can be real
    May success find its way to your hearts
Tomorrow can bring you the greatest of joys
    But today is the day it all starts.

ANONYMOUS

Song of the Open Road

Afoot and light-hearted I take to the open road,
Healthy, free, the world before me,
The long brown path before me leading wherever I choose.
Henceforth I ask not good-fortune – I myself am good-fortune;
Henceforth I whimper no more, postpone no more, need
    nothing,
Strong and content I travel the open road.

I inhale great draughts of space,
The east and the west are mine, and the north and the south
    are mine.
I am larger, better than I thought;
I did not know I held so much goodness.
All seems beautiful to me.

However sweet these laid-up stores – however convenient this
    dwelling, we cannot remain here.
However shelter'd the port, and however calm the waters, we
    must not anchor here,
However welcome the hospitality that surrounds us, we are
    permitted to receive it but a little while.

Listen! I will be honest with you,
I do not offer the old smooth prizes, but offer rough new
    prizes,
These are the days that must happen to you:
You shall not heap up what is call'd riches,
You shall scatter with lavish hand all that you earn or achieve.

My friend, I give you my hand!
I give you my love more precious than money,
I give you myself before preaching or law;
Will you give me yourself? Will you come travel with me?
Shall we stick by each other as long as we live?

WALT WHITMAN (1819–1892)

Our Love

Our love is something we have built
From passions, hopes and dreams.
It's safe from any passing moods,
Secure from all extremes.
It's something real and special,
Something solid, something pure.
It's something we can always count on,
Ringing sound and sure.
It's something grounded in the heart,
Emitting confidence.
It lives in our emotions;
It is something we can sense.
Our love remains a binding force,
Resistant to all strife.
Amidst the outer pressures,
It's our anchor throughout life.

BRUCE B. WILMER

The Gift of Love

Love is perfect tenderness,
A glance, a certain smile.
Love is understanding
And forgiving others too.
Love lies within us all
If we allow it to,
And perfect love encompasses
Each thing that we can do.
Love is simple yet complex;
It's selfless and extreme.
Yet love is adoration
And can also reign supreme.
Love can be unrequited
And this love causes pain
But when love is returned in full
Our spirits rise again.
The love we share throughout our lives
With someone by our side
Is one of such perfection
It cannot be described.
So when we have this gift of love
Be thankful every day
And always find within your life
A moment to convey
The way you feel about the love
You hold within your heart
For it isn't there for everyone
But a gift that is set apart.

JUDITH CALVER

A Third Body

A man and a woman sit near each other
and they do not long, at this moment
to be older, or younger, nor born in any other nation
or time or place.

They are content to be where they are,
talking or not talking.
Their breaths together feed someone whom we do not know.

The man sees the way his fingers move;
he sees her hands close around a book she hands to him.
They obey a third body that they share in common.
They have made a promise to love that body.

Age may come, parting may come, death will come.
A man and a woman sit near each other;
as they breathe they feed someone we do not know,
someone we know of, whom we have never seen.

ROBERT BLY (B 1926)
From *Loving a Woman in Two Worlds*

A Walled Garden

'Your marriage,' he said, 'should have within it, a secret and
    protected place open to you alone.
'Imagine it to be a walled garden, entered by a door to which
    you only hold the key.
'Within this garden you will cease to be a mother, father,
    employee, homemaker or any other of the roles which you
    fulfil in daily life.
'Here you are yourselves – two people, who love each other.
'Here you can concentrate on one another's needs.'

And so we made our walled garden.
Time that was kept for us alone.
At first we went there often, enjoying each other's company,
    sharing secrets, growing closer.
But now our days are packed with plans and people.
Conversation has become a message scribbled on a pad.
The door into our garden is almost hidden by rank weeds of
    busy-ness.
We claim we have no time because we have forgotten.
Forgotten that love grows if it is tended, and if neglected, dies.

But we can always make the time for what is most important
    in our lives.
So take my hand and let us go back to our garden.
The time we spend together is not wasted but invested.
Invested in our future and the nurture of our love.

ANONYMOUS

Take Time

Take time to THINK
       it is the source of power.
Take time to PLAY
       it is the secret of perpetual youth.
Take time to READ
       it is the fountain of wisdom.
Take time to PRAY
       it is the greatest power on earth.
Take time to LOVE and BE LOVED
       it is God's greatest gift.
Take time to BE FRIENDLY
       it is the road to happiness.
Take time to LAUGH
       it is the music of the soul.
Take time to GIVE
       it is too short a day to be selfish.
Take time to WORK
       it is the price of success.
Take time to BE CHARITABLE
       it is the key to heaven.

ANONYMOUS

Love

Love cannot be defined in one single term,
It cannot be taught and cannot be measured.
It should always be handled carefully,
An eternal and precious gift to always be treasured.
Love is fickle, love is kind,
It can only be bought by the heart.
Love sometimes makes you suffer,
It makes you cry when you're apart.
You cannot help who you love,
Nor can you make one love another.
Love is gentle and caring,
As is the love of a loving brother.
It cannot be taken lightly,
Those who pretend have much to learn.
Pompous airs accomplish nothing,
In the long run there's nothing in return.
One may die or one may leave,
Leaving others in despair.
But true love will never end,
As long as both continue to care.
So you get a taste of love,
It's gentle, kind and fair.
It's eternally remembered …
Lifting spirits when in despair.

REDDY FOX

The Art of a Good Marriage

Happiness in marriage is not something that just happens.
A good marriage must be created.
In marriage the little things are the big things:
It is never being too old to hold hands.
It is remembering to say 'I love you' at least once a day.
It is never going to sleep angry.
It is at no time taking the other for granted; the courtship
    should not end with the honeymoon, it should continue
    through all the years.
It is having a mutual sense of values and common objectives.
It is standing together facing the world.
It is forming a circle of love that gathers in the whole family.
It is doing things for each other, not in the attitude of duty or
    sacrifice, but in the spirit of joy.
It is speaking words of appreciation and demonstrating
    gratitude in thoughtful ways.
It is not expecting the husband to wear a halo or the wife to
    have the wings of an angel.
It is not looking for perfection in each other.
It is cultivating flexibility, patience, understanding and a sense
    of humour.
It is having the capacity to forgive and forget.
It is giving each other an atmosphere in which each can grow.
It is a common search for the good and the beautiful.
It is establishing a relationship in which the independence is
    equal, dependence is mutual and the obligation is reciprocal.
It is not only marrying the right partner, it is being the right
    partner.

WILFRED ARIAN PETERSON

To My Bride

To my bride, I give you my heart
    Sharing love each day, from the very start
To my bride, I give you my kiss
    Filling each day with joy and bliss
To my bride, I give you my being
    To love, to play, to work and to sing
To my bride, I give my mind
    Learning each day to be more kind
To my bride, I give you my soul
    Growing together to be more whole
To my bride, I give you my life
    Rejoicing each day that you are my wife.

STEVEN REISER

Positive Count

Count your blessings instead of your crosses;
    Count your gains instead of your losses;
Count your joys instead of your woes;
    Count your friends instead of your foes;
Count your courage instead of your fears;
    Count your laughs instead of your tears;
Count your full years instead of your lean;
    Count your kind deeds instead of your mean;
Count your health instead of your wealth;
    Count on God instead of yourself.

ANONYMOUS

Life's Lessons

After a while
You learn the difference
Between holding a hand
And chaining a soul.
You learn that love isn't leaning,
But lending support.
You begin to accept your defeats
With the grace of an adult,
Not the grief of a child.

You decide to build
Your roads on today,
For tomorrow's ground
Is too uncertain.
You help someone to plant a garden
Instead of waiting
For someone to bring you flowers.
You learn that God has given you
The strength to endure,
And that you really do have worth.

ANONYMOUS
Based on *After a while* by Veronica A. Shoffstall

Looking for Your Face

From the beginning of my life
I have been looking for your face
but today I have seen it

Today I have seen
The charm, the beauty,
The unfathomable grace
Of the face
That I was looking for

Today I have found you
and those who laughed
and scorned me yesterday
are sorry that they were not looking
as I did

I am bewildered by the magnificence
of your beauty
and wish to see you
with a hundred eyes

My heart has burned with passion
and has searched forever
for this wondrous beauty that I now behold

I am ashamed
to call this love human
and afraid of God
to call it divine

Your fragrant breath
like the morning breeze
has come to the stillness of the garden
You have breathed new life into me
I have become your sunshine
and also your shadow

My soul is screaming in ecstasy
Every fibre of my being
is in love with you
Your effulgence
has lit a fire in my heart
and you have made radiant
for me
the earth and sky

My arrow of love has arrived at the target
I am in the house of mercy
and my heart
is a place of prayer

JABAL AD-DIN AR-RUMI (1207–1273)
Translated from the Persian by Fereydoun Kia

Give All to Love

Give all to love;
Obey thy heart;
Friends, kindred, days,
Estate, good-fame,
Plans, credit and the Muse,
Nothing refuse.

'Tis a brave master;
Let it have scope:
Follow it utterly,
Hope beyond hope:
High and more high
It dives into noon,
With wing unspent,
Untold intent;
But it is a god,
Knows its own path
And the outlets of the sky.

It was never for the mean;
It requireth courage stout.
Souls above doubt,
Valour unbending.
It will reward,
They shall return
More than they were,
And ever ascending ...

RALPH WALDO EMERSON (1803–1882)

Reprise

Geniuses of countless nations
Have told their love for generations
Till all their memorable phrases
Are common as goldenrod or daisies.
Their girls have glimmered like the moon,
Or shimmered like a summer moon.
Stood like a lily, fled like a fawn,
Now the sunset, now the dawn,
Here the princess in the tower
There the sweet forbidden flower.
Darling, when I look at you
Every aged phrase is new,
And there are moments when it seems
I've married one of Shakespeare's dreams.

OGDEN NASH (1902–1971)

Today

Today I marry my friend,
the one I laugh and cry with,
the one I have learned from and shared with.

This one I have chosen to support,
encourage and give myself to,
through all the days given us to share.
Today I marry the one I love.

ANONYMOUS

Advice on Love and Marriage

You must follow the philosophy that men and women are
    equal and not treat either person with inferiority in any
    way.
You must be together always in your heart but not necessarily
    always in your activities.
You must be proud of each other and love and not be ashamed
    to show your sensitive feelings.
You must treat every day spent with each other as special and
    not take each other or your love for granted.
You must spend time talking with each other every day and
    not be too busy with outside events that you are too tired
    for each other.
You must understand each other's moods and feelings and not
    hurt each other intentionally but if your frustrations are
    taken out on each other you must both realize that it is not
    a personal attack.
You must be passionate with each other often and not get into
    boring patterns.
You must continue to have fun and excitement with each
    other and not be afraid to try new things.
You must always work at love and your love relationship and
    not forget how important this relationship is or what you
    would feel like without it.
Love is the strongest and most fulfilling emotion possible.
You will be living your dreams between awakenings if you
    culminate your commitment to love with marriage.

SUSAN POLIS SCHULTZ

Partners

The first dance of all when they danced heart to heart
    They knew, they both knew, it was only the start
Of something more wonderful than a mere dance
    More than a thrill of a passing romance.

They knew without saying that Love, the real thing,
    Had touched them that night with its shimmering wing.
No word had been spoken and yet they both knew
    That suddenly all sorts of dreams had come true.

It's many a year since the night that they met
    But that first dance they will never forget
Then a boy and a girl and now husband and wife
    Still happy, still dancing and partners for life.

PATIENCE STRONG (1907–1990)

All Things Are Ours

All things are ours because we love
The earth below, the sky above,
The mountains, meadow, sand and sea.
All things surrounding you and me
Are but a sweet reflection of
The gentle wonder of our love.

BARBARA BURROW

Seasons Come, Seasons Go

Seasons come, seasons go,
    moon-struck tides will ebb and flow;
when I forget my constant one
    he draws me back, he brings me home.
O love, my love, I hear you far away,
    a distant storm that will refresh the day.

Seasons come, seasons go,
    petals fall though flowers grow;
and when I doubt love lifts a hand
    and scatters stars like grains of sand.
Oh love, my love, I see you passing by
    like birds that fearlessly possess the sky.

Seasons come, seasons go,
    times to reap and times to sow;
but you are love, a fruitful vine,
    in ev'ry season yielding wine.
I hear my love in laughter and in song,
    no day too short, no winter night too long.

MICHAEL COCKETT

Love Is Giving

Love is giving, not taking,
mending, not breaking,
trusting, believing,
never deceiving,
patiently bearing
and faithfully sharing
each joy, every sorrow,
today and tomorrow.

Love is kind, understanding,
but never demanding.
Love is constant, prevailing,
its strength never failing.
A promise once spoken
for all time unbroken,
a lifetime together,
love's time is for ever.

ANONYMOUS

A Good Wedding Cake

4 lb of love
½ lb of good looks
1 lb sweet temper
1 lb butter of youth
1 lb of blindness of faults
1 lb of self-forgetfulness
1 lb of pounded wit
1 lb of good humour
2 tablespoons of sweet argument
1 pint of rippling laughter
1 wine glass of common sense
1 oz of modesty

Put the love, good looks and sweet temper into a well-
furnished house. Beat the butter of youth to a cream, and mix
well together with the blindness of faults and self-forgetfulness.
Stir the pounded wit and good humour into the sweet
argument, then add the rippling laughter, common sense and
modesty. Work the whole together until everything is well
mixed, and bake gently forever.

ANONYMOUS

Today I Married My Best Friend

Today I married my best friend,
Our bond is complete, it hath no end,
We share one soul, we share one heart,
A perfect time – a perfect start.

With these rings we share together,
Love so close to last forever,
This special day – two special hearts,
Let nothing keep this love apart.

RACHEL ELIZABETH COOPER (B 1977)

A Marriage Is a Promise

A marriage is a promise
That two hearts gladly make.
A promise to be tender,
To help, to give and take.
A marriage is a promise
To be kind and understanding
To be thoughtful and considerate,
Fair and undemanding.
A marriage is a promise
To share one life together …
A love-filled promise meant to be
Kept lovingly for ever.

ANONYMOUS

Oh Tell Me the Truth about Love

Some say that love's a little boy,
    And some say it's a bird,
Some say it makes the world go round,
    And some say that's absurd.
And when I asked the man next-door,
    Who looked as if he knew,
His wife got very cross indeed,
    And said it wouldn't do.

Does it look like a pair of pyjamas,
    Or the ham in a temperance hotel?
Does its odour remind one of llamas,
    Or has it a comforting smell?
Is it prickly to touch as a hedge is,
    Or soft as eiderdown fluff?
Is it sharp or quite smooth at the edges?
    O tell me the truth about love.

Our history books refer to it
    In cryptic little notes,
It's quite a common topic on
    The Transatlantic boats;
I've found the subject mentioned in
    Accounts of suicides,
And even seen it scribbled on
    The backs of railway-guides.

Does it howl like a hungry Alsatian,
    Or boom like a military band?
Could one give a first-rate imitation
    On a saw or a Steinway Grand?

Is its singing at parties a riot?
    Does it only like Classical stuff?
Will it stop when one wants to be quiet?
    O tell me the truth about love.

I looked inside the summer-house;
    It wasn't ever there:
I tried the Thames at Maidenhead,
    And Brighton's bracing air.
I don't know what the blackbird sang,
    Or what the tulip said;
But it wasn't in the chicken-run,
    Or underneath the bed.

Can it pull extraordinary faces?
    Is it usually sick on a swing?
Does it spend all its time at the races,
    Or fiddling with pieces of string?
Has it views of its own about money?
    Does it think Patriotism enough?
Are its stories vulgar but funny?
    O tell me the truth about love.

When it comes, will it come without warning
    Just as I'm picking my nose?
Will it knock on my door in the morning,
    Or tread in the bus on my toes?
Will it come like a change in the weather?
    Will its greeting be courteous or rough?
Will it alter my life altogether?
    O tell me the truth about love.

W.H. Auden (1907–1973)

Autumn Love

Spring love is daffodil-sharp;
Summer love is gaudy.
What image for Autumn?
A few rattling raspberry canes?
Dahlias, frost-warped?
Dried leaves whispering in hedgerows?

You walk through incandescent beechwoods,
Knee-deep in leaf-drift,
Hands purple with blackberry-harvest.
Your friends warm themselves
At the bonfire's white heat,
Their backs turned
Against the oncoming winter.

JEAN CARDY

I Will Be Here

If in the morning when you wake,
If the sun does not appear,
I will be here.
If in the dark we lose sight of love,
Hold my hand and have no fear,
I will be here.

I will be here,
When you feel like being quiet,
When you need to speak your mind I will listen.
Through the winning, losing, and trying we'll be together,
And I will be here.
If in the morning when you wake,
If the future is unclear,
I will be here.
As sure as seasons were made for change,
Our lifetimes were made for years,
I will be here.

I will be here,
And you can cry on my shoulder,
When the mirror tells us we're older.
I will hold you, to watch you grow in beauty,
And tell you all the things you are to me.
We'll be together and I will be here.
I will be true to the promises I've made,
To you and to the one who gave you to me.
I will be here.

STEVEN CURTIS CHAPMAN (B 1962)

Take a pinch of lovers' dreams
    Add a tender smile or two
One spoonful of tenderness
    And wishes fond and true
Throw in faithfulness and trust
    Simmer a decade or two
Then serve as loving friendship
    To last a lifetime through.

JUDITH CALVER

Guide for a Loving Home

May we treat one another
with respect, honesty and care.
May we share the little discoveries
and changes each day brings.
May we try always to be sensitive
to one another's joys, sorrows,
needs and changing moods,
and realise that being
a loving family means
sometimes not understanding
everyone all the time
but being there to love
and help them just the same.

ANONYMOUS

Love Poem

Yours is the face that the earth turns to me.
Continuous beyond its human features lie
The mountain forms that rest against the sky.
With your eyes, the reflecting rainbow, the sun's light
Sees me, forest and flowers, bird and beast
Know and hold me forever in the world's thought,
Creation's deep untroubled retrospect.

When your hand touches mine, it is the earth
That takes me – the deep grass
And rocks and rivers; the green graves,
And children still unborn, and ancestors,
In love passed down from hand to hand from God.
Your love comes from the creation of the world,
From those paternal fingers, streaming through the clouds
That break with light the surface of the sea.

Here, where I trace your body with my hand,
Love's presence has no end;
For these, your arms that hold me, are the world's
In us, the continents, clouds and oceans meet
Our arbitrary selves, extensive with the night,
Lost, in the heart's worship, and the body's sleep.

KATHLEEN RAINE (B 1908)

And When I Thought

And when I thought how my dear friend my lover was on his
way coming, O then I was happy,

O then each breath tasted sweeter, and all that day my food
nourish'd me more, and the beautiful day pass'd well,

And the next came with equal joy, and with the next at
evening came my friend,

And that night while all was still I heard the waters roll
slowly continually up the shores,

I heard the hissing rustle of the liquid and sands as directed to
me whispering to congratulate me,

For the one I love most lay sleeping by me under the same
cover in the cool night,

In the stillness in the autumn moonbeams his face was
inclined toward me,

And his arm lay lightly around my breast – and that night I
was happy.

WALT WHITMAN (1819–1892)
From *When I Heard at the Close of the Day*

Why Marriage?

Because to the depths of me, I long to love one person,
With all my heart, my soul, my mind, my body …
Because I need a forever friend to trust with the intimacies of me,
Who won't hold them against me,
Who loves me when I'm unlikable,
Who sees the small child in me, and
Who looks for the divine potential of me …
Because I need to cuddle in the warmth of the night
With someone who thanks God for me,
With someone I feel blessed to hold …
Because marriage means opportunity
To grow in love in friendship …
Because marriage is a discipline
To be added to a list of achievements…
Because marriages do not fail, people fail
When they enter into marriage
Expecting another to make them whole …
Because, knowing this,
I promise myself to take full responsibility
For my spiritual, mental and physical wholeness,
I create me,
I take half of the responsibility for my marriage,
Together we create our marriage …
Because with this understanding
The possibilities are limitless.

ANONYMOUS

Yes, I'll Marry You

Yes, I'll marry you, my dear,
And here's the reason why;
So I can push you out of bed
When the baby starts to cry,
And if we hear a knocking
And it's creepy and it's late,
I hand you the torch, you see,
And you investigate.

Yes I'll marry you, my dear,
You may not apprehend it,
But when the tumble-drier goes
It's you that has to mend it,
And if a drunkard fondles me
It's you that has to whack him.

Yes, I'll marry you,
You're virile and you're lean,
My house is like a pigsty
You can help to keep it clean.
That sexy little dinner
Which you served by candlelight,
As I do chipolatas,
You can cook it every night!

It's you who has to work the drill
And put up curtain track,
And when I've got PMT
It's you who gets the flak,

I do see great advantages,
But none of them for you,
And so before you see the light,
I do, I do, I do!

PAM AYRES (B 1947)

True Love

True love is a sacred flame
That burns eternally,
And none can dim its special glow
Or change its destiny.
True love speaks in tender tones
And hears with gentle ear,
True love gives with open heart
And true love conquers fear.
True love makes no harsh demands
It neither rules nor binds,
And true love holds with gentle hands
The hearts that it entwines.

ANONYMOUS

What Is Love?

Not everyone has love at first sight
Personality counts then you know it is right,

First is the glance of eyes across the room
As if you are flowers waiting to bloom,

Your body shakes as you move another pace,
Your hands all sweaty and your heart in a race,

The first word you speak seems to echo around,
All eyes gazing waiting for the spoken word to make a sound,

All you can hear as you lay the first kiss,
Is your heart giving a sigh of heavenly bliss.

SHERREE LOUISE HAMBLYN

i carry your heart with me

i carry your heart with me(i carry it in
my heart)i am never without it(anywhere
i go you go, my dear;and whatever is done
by only me is your doing,my darling)
                        i fear
no fate(for you are my fate,my sweet)i want
no world(for beautiful you are my world,my true)
and it's you are whatever a moon has always meant
and whatever a sun will always sing is you

here is the deepest secret nobody knows
(here is the root of the root and the bud of the bud
and the sky of the sky of a tree called life;which grows
higher than soul can hope or mind can hide)
and this is the wonder that's keeping the stars apart

i carry your heart(i carry it in my heart)

E.E. Cummings (1894–1962)

What Almost Every Woman Knows Sooner or Later

Husbands are things that wives have to get used to putting up
   with.
And with whom they breakfast with and sup with.
They interfere with the discipline of nurseries,
And forget anniversaries,
And when they have been particularly remiss
They think they can cure everything with a great big kiss,
And when you tell them about something awful they have
   done they just look unbearably patient and smile a superior
   smile,
And think, Oh she'll get over it after a while.
And they always drink cocktails faster than they can assimilate
   them,
And if you look in their direction they act as if they were
   martyrs and you were trying to sacrifice, or immolate
   them,
And when it's a question of walking five miles to play golf
   they are very energetic but if it's doing anything useful
   around the house they are very lethargic,
And then they tell you that women are unreasonable and
   don't know anything about logic,
And they never want to get up or go to bed at the same time
   as you do,
And when you perform some simple common or garden rite
   like putting cold cream on your face or applying a touch of
   lipstick they seem to think that you are up to some kind of
   black magic like a priestess of Voodoo.
And they are brave and calm and cool and collected about the
   ailments of the person they have promised to honor and
   cherish,

But the minute they get a sniffle or a stomach-ache of their
  own, why you'd think they were about to perish,
And when you are alone with them they ignore all the minor
  courtesies and as for airs and graces, they utterly lack them,
But when there are a lot of people around they hand you so
  many chairs and ashtrays and sandwiches and butter you
  with such bowings and scrapings that you want to smack
  them.
Husbands are indeed an irritating form of life,
And yet through some quirk of Providence most of them are
  really very deeply ensconced in the affection of their wife.

OGDEN NASH (1902–1971)

These I Can Promise

I cannot promise you a life of sunshine;
I cannot promise riches, wealth, or gold;
I cannot promise you an easy pathway
That leads away from change or growing old.

But I can promise all my heart's devotion;
A smile to chase away your tears of sorrow;
A love that's ever true and ever growing;
A hand to hold in yours through each tomorrow.

ANONYMOUS

This Day I Married My Best Friend

This day I married my best friend
    … the one I laugh with as we share life's wondrous zest,
as we find new enjoyments and experience all that's best.
    … the one I live for because the world seems brighter
as our happy times are better and our burdens feel much lighter.
    … the one I love with every fibre of my soul.
We used to feel vaguely incomplete, now together we are whole.

ANONYMOUS

The Colour of My Love

I'll paint a sun to warm your heart
Knowing that we'll never part.
I'll draw the years all passing by
So much to learn, so much to try.

I'll paint my mood in shadow blue,
Paint my soul to be with you.
I'll sketch your lips in shaded tones,
Draw your mouth to my own.

I'll trace a hand to wipe your tears
I'll trace a look to calm your fears.
A silhouette of dark and light
To hold each other oh so tight.

I'll paint the stars in the evening sky,
Draw the light into your eyes,
A touch of love, a touch of grace,
To softly fall on your moonlit face.

And with this ring our lives will start,
Let nothing keep our love apart.
I'll take your hand to hold in mine,
And be together through all time.

DAVID FOSTER AND ARTHUR JANOV

To Keep Your Marriage Brimming

To keep your marriage brimming,
With love in the loving cup,
Whenever you're wrong admit it;
Whenever you're right shut up.

OGDEN NASH (1902–1971)

Give Me Your Heart

Give me your heart, beloved. Give me your hand, my true
   friend.
With each passing day I grow more fond;
With each passing day, our small portion of love takes its place
   in the truth of time.
With the years that we have been given,
Let us grow deeply into life so that we may love all the more.

ANONYMOUS

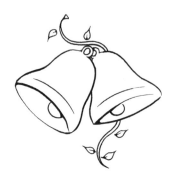

The Heart's Anchor

Think of me as your friend, I pray,
And call me by a loving name;
I will not care what others say,
If only you will remain the same.
I will not care how dark the night,
I will not care how wild the storm,
Your love will fill my heart with light
And shield me close and keep me warm.

WILLIAM WINTER (1836–1917)

A White Rose

The red rose whispers of passion,
And the white rose breathes of love;
O the red rose is a falcon,
And the white rose is a dove.

But I send you a cream-white rosebud
With a flush on its petal tips;
For the love that is purest and sweetest
Has a kiss of desire on the lips.

JOHN BOYLE O'REILLY (1844–1890)

Because

Because we have things in common, we have the joy of
    sharing them.
Because we are so different, there is so much we can learn
    from each other.
Because we love each other, we look for the good in the other.
Because we are forgiving, we overlook the faults in each other.
Because we are patient, we give each other time to
    understand.
Because we are filled with kindness, we compliment the
    things we do for each other.
Because we can empathize, we know what it's like to stand in
    each other's shoes.
Because we have character, we enjoy each other's uniqueness.
Because we have faith, we believe the best for the future.
Because we are honest, we are comfortable to trust each other.
Because we are filled with loyalty, we always know the other
    will be there.

STEVEN REISER

Love's Coming

Quietly as rosebuds
Talk to the thin air,
Love came so lightly,
I knew not he was there.

Quietly as lovers
Creep at the middle moon,
Softly as players tremble
In the tears of a tune;

Quietly as lilies
Their faint vows declare
Came the shy pilgrim:
I knew not he was there.

Quietly as tears fall
On a warm sin,
Softly as griefs call
In a violin;

Without hail or tempest,
Blue sword of flame.
Love came so lightly
I knew not that he came.

ANONYMOUS

The Key to Love

The key to love is understanding ...
> The ability to comprehend not only the spoken word,
> but those unspoken gestures,
> the little things that say so much by themselves.

The key to love is forgiveness ...
> To accept each other's faults and pardon mistakes,
> without forgetting, but with remembering
> what you learn from them.

The key to love is sharing ...
> Facing your good fortunes as well as the bad, together;
> both conquering problems, forever searching for ways
> to intensify your happiness.

The key to love is giving ...
> Without thought of return,
> but with the hope of just a simple smile,
> and by giving in but never giving up.

The key to love is respect ...
> Realising that you are two separate people, with different
> ideas;
> that you don't belong to each other,
> that you belong with each other, and share a mutual bond.

The key to love is inside us all ...
   It takes time and patience to unlock all the ingredients that
   will take you to its threshold;
   it is the continual learning process that demands a lot of
   work ...
   but the rewards are more than worth the effort ...
   and that is the key to love.

ANONYMOUS

The Confirmation

Yes, yours, my love, is the right human face.
I in my mind had waited for this long,
Seeing the false and searching for the true,
Then found you as a traveller finds a place
Of welcome suddenly amid the wrong
Valleys and rocks and twisting roads. But you,
What shall I call you? A fountain in a waste,
A well of water in a country dry,
Or anything that's honest and good, an eye
That makes the whole world bright. Your open heart,
Simple with giving, gives the primal deed,
The first good world, the blossom, the blowing seed,
The hearth, the steadfast land, the wandering sea.
Not beautiful or rare in every part.
But like yourself, as they were meant to be.

EDWIN MUIR (1887–1959)

The Place

The place whence comes each happy inspiration ...
Where love serenely dwells ... and hope is born ...
Where strivings cease ... and strife is barred the door.
Where confidence is bred ... and the eloquence of silence
    understood.
A place where plans are made and journeys start,
Where journeys end in happy welcomings.

Where dwells that peace so eagerly desired by all ...
And mutual trust survives whate'er befall.
Where laughter is not very far away, and truth is reverenced.
Where friends drop in to share our joys or woes,
And absent friends are ever in our thoughts.
God give you such a home.

ANONYMOUS

Love Does Not Consist in Gazing at One Another

Love does not consist in gazing at one another,
But in looking outward together in the same direction.
Do not seek perfection in each other.
Do not seek to make the other into your own image,
or to remake yourself into another's image.
What each most truly is will be known by the other.
It is that truth of you which must be loved.
Many things will change, but change is not the enemy of love.
Change is the enemy only of any attempt to possess.
May all that is good and true and beautiful
Abide with you now and always.

ANONYMOUS

American Indian Wedding Blessing

Now you will feel no rain,
    for each of you will be shelter to the other.
Now you will feel no cold,
    for each of you will be warmth to the other.
Now you will feel no loneliness,
    for each of you will be companionship to the other.
Now you are two persons,
    but there are three lives before you: his life, her life and
    your life together.

Go now to your dwelling place,
    to enter into the days of your life together.
May beauty surround you both in the journey ahead
    and through all the years may happiness be your
    companion to the place where the river meets the sun,
And may your days be good and long upon the earth.

Treat yourselves and each other with respect,
And remind yourselves often of what brought you together.
Give the highest priority to the tenderness,
    gentleness and kindness that your connection deserves.
When frustration, difficulty and fear assail your relationship –
    as they threaten all relationships at one time or another –
    remember to focus on what is right between you, not only
    that part which seems wrong.
In this way, you can ride out the storms
    when clouds hide the face of the sun in your lives.

TRADITIONAL AMERICAN INDIAN

Apache Blessing

May the sun bring you new energy by day,
May the moon softly restore you by night,
May the rain wash away your worries
And the breeze blow new strength into your being,
And all of the days of your life may you walk
Gently through the world and know its beauty.

TRADITIONAL APACHE

Hindu Marriage Poem

You have become mine forever.
Yes, we have become partners.
I have become yours.
Hereafter, I cannot live without you.
Do not live without me.
Let us share the joys.
We are word and meaning, unite.
You are thought and I am sound.
May the nights be honey-sweet for us.
May the mornings be honey-sweet for us.
May the plants be honey-sweet for us.
May the earth be honey-sweet for us.

TRADITIONAL HINDU

An Irish Blessing

May the road rise to meet you,
May the wind be always at your back.
May the sun shine warm upon your face,
The rains fall soft upon your fields.
And until we meet again,
May God hold you in the palm of His hand.

May God be with you and bless you;
May you see your children's children.
May you be poor in misfortune,
Rich in blessings,
May you know nothing but happiness
From this day forward.

May the road rise to meet you
May the wind be always at your back
May the warm rays of sun fall upon your home
And may the hand of a friend always be near.
May green be the grass you walk on,
May blue be the skies above you,
May pure be the joys that surround you,
May true be the hearts that love you.

TRADITIONAL IRISH

Eskimo Love Song

You are my husband/wife
My feet shall run because of you
My feet dance because of you
My heart shall beat because of you
My eyes see because of you
My mind thinks because of you
And I shall love because of you.

TRADITIONAL ESKIMO

Go Deeper than Love

Go deeper than love, for the soul has greater depths,
love is like the grass, but the heart is deep wild rock
molten, yet dense and permanent.
Go down to your deep old heart, and lose sight of yourself.
And lose sight of me, the me whom you turbulently love.
Let us lose sight of ourselves, and break the mirrors.
For the fierce curve of our lives is moving again to the depths
Out of sight, in the deep living heart.

D.H. LAWRENCE (1885–1930)
From *Know Deeply, Know Thyself More Deeply*

Blessing for a Wedding

From the east I come to offer blessings
    For the powers of the wind, I wish you wisdom in hardship,
    laughter in joy, trust in each other.
    I offer blessings over all beginnings you ever choose
    together,
    and the brightness of all dawning times.
    Under the overarching sky, I offer blessings,
    in the name of all teachers.

From the south I come to offer blessings
    For the powers of the fire, I wish you strength over grimness,
    light in darkness, pride in each other.
    I offer blessings over all things you are passionate in together,
    and the warmth of flame in the joining of your souls.
    Under the glory of our sun, I offer blessings,
    in the name of all guardians.

From the west I come to offer blessings
    For the powers of the sea, I wish you compassion in grief,
    patience in frustration, delight in each other.
    I offer blessings over all laughter you share together
    and the calm of the eternal waves under moonlight.
    Above the sparkle of the oceans, I offer blessings
    in the name of all lovers.

From the north I come to offer blessings
    For the powers of the mountain, I wish you fortitude in delay,
    beauty in stillness, support in each other.
    I offer blessings over all things lasting you hold together
    and the glow at the heart of an amber.
    Above the eternity of the rising earth, I offer blessings
    in the name of all heroes.

From within I come to offer blessings
    For the powers of those without, I wish you delight in life
    diversity in unity, love always.
    I offer blessings over all companions travelled with together
    and true hearts to share unstintingly.
    In heartfelt love and delight, I offer blessings
    in the name of all friends.

ANNE CROSS

I Do, I Will, I Have

How wise I am to have instructed the butler to instruct the
    first footman to instruct the second footman to instruct the
    doorman to order my carriage;
I am about to volunteer a definition of marriage.
Just as I know that there are two Hagens, Walter and Copen,
I know that marriage is a legal and religious alliance entered
    into by a man who can't sleep with the window shut and a
    woman who can't sleep with the window open.
Moreover, just as I am unsure of the difference between flora
    and fauna and flotsam and jetsam,
I am quite sure that marriage is the alliance of two people one
    of whom never remembers birthdays and the other never
    forgetsam,
And he refuses to believe there is a leak in the water pipe or
    the gas pipe and she is convinced she is about to asphyxiate
    or drown,
And she says Quick get up and get my hairbrushes off the
    windowsill, it's raining in, and he replies Oh they're all
    right, it's only raining straight down.
That is why marriage is so much more interesting than
    divorce,
Because it's the only known example of the happy meeting of
    the immovable object and the irresistible force.
So I hope husbands and wives will continue to debate and
    combat over everything debatable and compatible,
Because I believe a little incompatibility is the spice of life,
    particularly if he has income and she is pattable.

OGDEN NASH (1902–1971)

*(Walter Hagen was golf's first superstar during the 1920s and 30s. Copen
Hagen is, of course, the capital of Denmark.)*

The Newly Wedded

Now the rite is duly done,
Now the word is spoken,
And the spell has made us one
Which may ne'er be broken:
Rest we, dearest, in our home,
Roam we o'er the heather,
We shall rest, and we shall roam,
Shall we not? together.

From this hour the summer rose
Sweeter breathes to charm us;
From this hour the winter snows
Lighter fall to harm us:
Fair or foul – on land or sea –
Come the wind or weather,
Best or worst, whate'er they be,
We shall share together.

WINTHROP MACKWORTH PRAED (1802–1839)

Sonnet from the Portuguese XIV

If thou must love me, let it be for nought
Except for love's sake only. Do not say
'I love her for her smile, her look, her way
Of speaking gently, for a trick of thought
That falls in well with mine, and certes brought
A sense of pleasant ease on such a day' –
For these things in themselves, Beloved, may
Be changed, or change for thee, and love, so wrought,
May be unwrought so. Neither love me for
Thine own dear pity's wiping my cheeks dry,
Since one might well forget to weep who bore
Thy comfort long, and lose they love thereby.
But love me for love's sake, that evermore
Thou may'st love on through love's eternity.

ELIZABETH BARRETT BROWNING (1806–1861)

Because She Would Ask Me Why I Loved Her

If questioning would make us wise
No eyes would ever gaze in eyes;
If all our tale were told in speech
No mouths would wander each to each.

Were spirits free from mortal mesh
And love not bound in hearts of flesh
No aching breasts would yearn to meet
And find their ecstasy complete.

For who is there that lives and knows
The secret powers by which he grows?
Were knowledge all, what were our need
To thrill and faint and sweetly bleed?

Then seek not, sweet, the 'If' and 'Why'
I love you now until I die.
For I must love because I live
And life in me is what you give.

CHRISTOPHER BRENNAN (1870–1932)

Kindliness

When love has changed to kindliness –
Oh, love, our hungry lips, that press
So tight that Time's an old god's dream
Nodding in heaven, and whisper stuff
Seven million years were not enough
To think on after, make it seem
Less than the breath of children playing,
A blasphemy scarce worth the saying,
A sorry jest, 'When love has grown
To kindliness – to kindliness!' . . .
And yet – the vest that either's known
Will change, and wither, and be less
At last, than comfort, or its own
Remembrance. And when some caress
Tendered in habit (once a flame
All heaven sang out to) wakes the shame
Unworried, in the steady eyes
We'll have – *that* day, what shall we do?
Being so noble, kill the two
Who've reached their second-best? Being wise,
Break cleanly off, and get away,
Follow down other windier skies
New lures, alone? Or shall we stay,
Since this is all we've known, content
In the lean twilight of such day,
And not remember, not lament?
That time when all is over, and
Hand never flinches, brushing hand;
And blood lies quiet, for all you're near;
And it's but spoken words we hear,

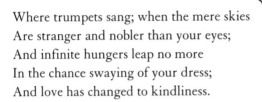

Where trumpets sang; when the mere skies
Are stranger and nobler than your eyes;
And infinite hungers leap no more
In the chance swaying of your dress;
And love has changed to kindliness.

RUPERT BROOKE (1887–1915)

A Dedication to My Wife

To whom I owe the leaping delight
That quickens my senses in our wakingtime
And the rhythm that governs the repose of our sleepingtime,
The breathing in unison

Of lovers whose bodies smell of each other
Who think the same thoughts without need of speech
And babble the same speech without need of meaning.

No peevish winter wind shall chill
No sullen tropic sun shall wither
The roses in the rose-garden which is ours and ours only

But this dedication is for others to read:
These are my private words addressed to you in public.

T.S. ELIOT (1888–1965)

Marriage

The die is cast, come weal, come woe,
Two lives are joined together,
For better or for worse, the link
Which naught but death can sever.
The die is cast, come grief, come joy.
Come richer, or come poorer,
If love but binds the mystic tie,
Blest is the bridal hour.

MARY WESTON FORDHAM (c1862–?)

Fidelity and Love

Fidelity and love are two different things, like a flower and a gem.
Man and woman are like the earth, that brings forth flowers
    in summer and love, but underneath is rock.
Older than flowers, older than ferns, older than foraminifera,
    older than plasma altogether is the soul underneath.
And when, throughout all the wild chaos of love
    slowly a gem forms, in the ancient, once-more-molten rocks,
Of two human hearts, two ancient rocks,
    a man's heart and a woman's,
That is the crystal of peace, the slow, hard jewel of trust,
    the sapphire of fidelity.
The gem of mutual peace emerging from the wild chaos
    of love.

D. H. LAWRENCE (1885–1930)

The Song of Love

How shall I guard my soul so that it be
Touched not by thine? And how shall it be brought,
Lifted above thee, into other things?
Ah, gladly would I hide it utterly
Lost in the dark where are no murmurings,
In strange and silent places that do not
Vibrate when the deep sail quivers and sings.
But all that touches us two makes us twin,
Even as the bow crossing the violin
Draws but one voice from the two strings that meet.
Upon what instrument are we two spanned?
And what great player has us in his hand?
O song most sweet.

RAINER MARIA RILKE (1875–1926)

On Marriage

You were born together, and together you shall be forevermore.
  You shall be together when white wings of death scatter
    your days.
  Aye, you shall be together even in the silent memory of
    God.
  But let there be spaces in your togetherness,
  And let the winds of the heavens dance between you.

Love one another but make not a bond of love:
  Let it rather be a moving sea between the shores of your
    souls.
  Fill each other's cup but drink not from one cup.
  Give one another of your bread but eat not from the same
    loaf.
  Sing and dance together and be joyous, but let each one of
    you be alone,
  Even as the strings of a lute are alone though they quiver
    with the same music.

Give your hearts, but not into each other's keeping.
  For only the hand of Life can contain your hearts.
  And stand together, yet not too near together:
  For the pillars of the temple stand apart,
  And the oak tree and the cypress grow not in each other's
    shadow.

KAHLIL GIBRAN (1883–1931)
From *The Prophet*

What Love Is

Love is the centre and circumference;
    The cause and aim of all things – 'tis the key
To joy and sorrow, and the recompense
    For all the ills that have been, or may be.

Love is as bitter as the dregs of sin,
    As sweet as clover-honey in its cell;
Love is the password whereby soul gets in
    To Heaven – the gate that leads, sometimes, to Hell.

Love is the crown that glorifies; the curse
    That brands and burdens; it is life and death.
It is the great law of the universe;
    And nothing can exist without its breath.

Love is the impulse which directs the world,
    And all things know it and obey its power.
Man, in the maelstrom of his passion whirled;
    The bee that takes the pollen to the flower;

The earth, uplifting her bare, pulsing breast
    To fervent kisses of the amorous sun;
Each but obeys creative Love's behest,
    Which everywhere instinctively is done.

Love is the only thing that pays for birth,
    Or makes death welcome. O dear God above
This beautiful but sad, perplexing earth,
    Pity the hearts that know – or know not – Love!

ELLA WHEELER WILCOX (1855–1919)

When You Are Old

When you are old and grey and full of sleep,
And nodding by the fire, take down this book,
And slowly read, and dream of the soft look
Your eyes had once, and of their shadows deep;

How many loved your moments of glad grace,
And loved your beauty with love false or true,
But one man loved the pilgrim soul in you,
And loved the sorrows of your changing face;

And bending down beside the glowing bars,
Murmur, a little sadly, how Love fled
And paced upon the mountains overhead
And hid his face amid a crowd of stars.

W.B. YEATS (1865–1939)

The Way That Lovers Use

The way that lovers use is this;
    They bow, catch hands, with never a word,
And their lips meet, and they do kiss,
    – So I have heard.

They queerly find some healing so,
    And strange attainment in the touch;
There is a secret lovers know,
    – I have read as much.

And theirs no longer joy nor smart,
    Changing or ending, night or day;
But mouth to mouth, and heart on heart,
    – So lovers say.

Rupert Brooke (1887–1915)

Love Much

Love much. There is no waste in freely giving;
More blessed is it, even, than to receive.
Love much. Earth has enough of bitter in it;
Cast sweets into its cup whene'er you can.
No heart so hard, but love at last may win it;
Love is the grand primeval cause of man;
All hate is foreign to the first great plan.

Love much. Your heart will be led out to slaughter,
On altars built of envy and deceit.
Love on, love on! 'tis bread upon the water;
It shall be cast in loaves yet at your feet,
Unleaven manna, most divinely sweet.

Love much. Your faith will be dethroned and shaken,
Your trust betrayed by many a fair, false lure.
Remount your faith, and let new trusts awaken.
Though clouds obscure them, yet the stars are pure;
Love is a vital force and must endure.

Love much. Men's souls contract with cold suspicion,
Shine on them with warm love, and they expand.
'Tis love, not creeds, that from a low condition
Leads mankind up to heights supreme and grand.
Oh, that the world could see and understand!

Love much. There is no waste in freely giving;
More blessed is it, even than to receive.
He who loves much, alone finds life worth living;
Love on, through doubt and darkness; and believe
There is no thing which Love may not achieve.

ELLA WHEELER WILCOX (1850–1919)

A Birthday

My heart is like a singing bird
    Whose nest is in a watered shoot;
My heart is like an apple-tree
    Whose boughs are bent with thick-set fruit;
My heart is like a rainbow shell
    That paddles in a halcyon sea;
My heart is gladder than all these
    Because my love is come to me.

Raise me a dais of silk and down;
    Hang it with vair and purple dyes;
Carve it in doves and pomegranates
    And peacocks with a hundred eyes;
Work it in gold and silver grapes,
    In leaves and silver fleurs-de-lys;
Because the birthday of my life
    Is come, my love is come to me.

CHRISTINA GEORGINA ROSSETTI (1830–1894)

A Description of Love

Now what is love, I pray thee tell?
It is that fountain and that well
Where pleasure and repentance dwell.
It is perhaps that sauncing bell
That tolls all into heaven or hell:
And this is love, as I hear tell.

Yet what is love, I pray thee say?
It is a work on holy day.
It is December matched with May,
When lusty bloods in fresh array
Hear ten months after of the play:
And this is love, as I hear say.

Yet what is love, I pray thee sain?
It is a sunshine mixed with rain.
It is a tooth-ache, or like pain;
It is a game where none doth gain;
The lass saith No, and would full fain;
And this is love, as I hear sain.

Yet what is love I pray thee say?
It is a yea, it is a nay,
A pretty kind of sporting fray;
It is a thing will soon away;
Then take the vantage while you may;
And this is love, as I hear say.

Yet what is love I pray thee show?
A thing that creeps, it cannot go;
A prize that passeth to and fro;
A thing for one, a thing for mo;
And he that proves must find it so:
And this is love, sweet friend, I trow.

SIR WALTER A. RALEIGH (1552–1618)

Married Love

Take a lump of clay, wet it, pat it,
And make an image of me, and an image of you.
Then smash them, crash them, and add a little water.
Break them and remake them into an image of you
And an image of me.
Then in my clay, there's a little of you.
And in your clay, there's a little of me.
And nothing ever shall us sever;
Living, we'll sleep in the same quilt,
And dead, we'll be buried together.

KUAN TAO-SHENG (1263–1319)

A Red, Red Rose

O, my Luve's like a red, red rose,
    That's newly sprung in June:
O my Luve's like the melodie
    That's sweetly play'd in tune.

As fair art thou, my bonnie lass,
    So deep in luve am I:
And I will love thee still, my Dear,
    Till a' the seas gang dry:

Till a' the seas gang dry, my Dear,
    And the rocks melt wi' the sun:
I will luve thee still, my Dear,
    While the sands o' life shall run.

And fare thee weel, my only Luve,
    And fare thee weel a while!
And I will come again, my Luve.
    Tho' it were ten thousand mile!

ROBERT BURNS (1759–1796)

Destiny

Somewhere there waiteth in this world of ours
For one lone soul another lonely soul,
Each choosing each through all the weary hours
And meeting strangely at one sudden goal.
Then blend they, like green leaves with golden flowers,
Into one beautiful and perfect whole;
And life's long night is ended, and the way
Lies open onward to eternal day.

SIR EDWIN ARNOLD (1832–1904)

We ...

We ... like two artificial gods,
Have with our needles created both one flower,
Both on one sampler, sitting on one cushion,
Both warbling of one song, both in one key,
As if our hands, our sides, voices and minds,
Had been incorporated. So we grew together,
Like to a double cherry, seeming parted,
But yet an union in partition;
Two lovely berries moulded on one stem;
So, with two seeming bodies, but one heart;
Two of the first, like coats in heraldry,
Due but to one and crowned with one crest.

WILLIAM SHAKESPEARE (1564–1616)
From *A Midsummer Night's Dream, Act III, Scene ii*

Now Sleeps the Crimson Petal

Now sleeps the crimson petal, now the white;
Nor waves the cypress in the palace walk;
Nor winks the gold fin in the porphyry font:
The fire-fly wakens: waken thou with me.

Now droops the milkwhite peacock like a ghost,
And like a ghost she glimmers on to me.

Now lies the earth all Danaë to the stars,
And all thy heart lies open unto me.

Now slides the silent meteor on, and leaves
A shining furrow, as thy thoughts in me.

Now folds the lily all her sweetness up,
And slips into the bosom of the lake:
So fold thyself, my dearest, thou, and slip
Into my bosom and be lost in me.

ALFRED, LORD TENNYSON (1809–1892)
From *The Princess, 7, Song 2*

I Love Thee

I love thee – I love thee!
'Tis all that I can say;
It is my vision in the night,
My dreaming in the day;
The very echo of my heart,
The blessing when I pray:
I love thee – I love thee!
Is all that I can say.

I love thee – I love thee!
Is ever on my tongue;
In all my proudest poesy
That chorus still is sung;
It is the verdict of my eyes,
Amidst the gay and young:
I love thee – I love thee!
A thousand maids among.

I love thee – I love thee!
Thy bright and hazel glance,
The mellow lute upon those lips,
Whose tender tones entrance;
But most, dear heart of hearts, thy proofs
That still these words enhance.
I love thee – I love thee!
Whatever be thy chance.

THOMAS HOOD (1799–1845)

Love Lives

Love lives beyond
The tomb, the earth, which fades like dew.
I love the fond,
The faithful, and the true.

Love lives in sleep,
The happiness of healthy dreams
Eve's dews may weep,
But love delightful seems.

'Tis heard in Spring
When light and sunbeams, warm and kind,
On angels' wing
Bring love and music to the mind.

And where is voice,
So young, so beautiful and sweet
As nature's choice,
Where Spring and lovers meet?

Love lives beyond
The tomb, the earth, the flowers, and dew.
I love the fond,
The faithful, young and true.

JOHN CLARE (1793–1864)

He Wishes for the Cloths of Heaven

Had I the heavens' embroidered cloths,
Enwrought with golden and silver light,
The blue and the dim and the dark cloths
Of night and light and the half-light,
I would spread the cloths under your feet:
But I, being poor, have only my dreams;
I have spread my dreams under your feet;
Tread softly because you tread on my dreams.

W.B. YEATS (1865–1959)

Love Rules

Love rules the court,
The camp, the grove,
And men below, and the saints above,
For love is heaven
And heaven is love.

SIR WALTER SCOTT (1771–1832)

Love's Philosophy

The fountains mingle with the river
And the rivers with the ocean,
The winds of heaven mix forever
With a sweet emotion;
Nothing in the world is single,
All things by a law divine
In one spirit meet and mingle –
Why not I with thine?

See the mountains kiss high heaven
And the waves clasp one another;
No sister-flower would be forgiven
If it disdained its brother:
And the sunlight clasps the earth
And the moonbeams kiss the sea –
What is all this sweet work worth
If thou kiss not me?

PERCY BYSSHE SHELLEY (1792–1822)

Marriage Morning

Light, so low upon earth,
You send a flash to the sun.
Here is the golden close of love,
All my wooing is done.
Oh, the woods and the meadows,
Woods where we hid from the wet,
Stiles where we stay'd to be kind,
Meadows in which we met!

Light, so low in the vale
You flash and lighten afar,
For this is the golden morning of love,
And you are his morning star.
Flash, I am coming, I come,
By meadow and stile and wood,
Oh, lighten into my eyes and heart,
Into my heart and my blood!

Heart, are you great enough
For a love that never tires?
O heart, are you great enough for love?
I have heard of thorns and briers.
Over the thorns and briers,
Over the meadows and stiles,
Over the world to the end of it
Flash for a million miles.

ALFRED, LORD TENNYSON (1809–1892)

On Love

Love has no other desire but to fulfil itself.
But if you love and must needs have desires, let these be your
  desires:
To melt and be like a running brook that sings its melody to
  the night.
To know the pain of too much tenderness.
To be wounded by your own understanding of love,
And to bleed willingly and joyfully.
To wake at dawn with a winged heart and give thanks for
  another day of loving;
To rest at the noon hour and meditate love's ecstasy;
To return home at eventide with gratitude;
And then to sleep with a prayer for the beloved in your heart
  and a song of praise on your lips.

KAHLIL GIBRAN (1883–1931)
From *The Prophet*

Oh No – Not Even When First We Loved

Oh, no – not ev'n when first we lov'd
Wert thou as dear as now thou art;
Thy beauty then my senses mov'd.
But now thy virtues bind my heart.
What was but Passion's sign before
Has since been turn'd to Reason's vow;
And, though I then might love thee more,
Trust me, I love thee better now.
Although my heart in earlier youth
Might kindle with more wild desire,
Believe me, it has gain'd in truth
Much more than it has lost in fire.
The flame now warms my inmost core
That then but sparkled o'er my brow,
And though I seem'd to love thee more,
Yet, oh, I love thee better now.

THOMAS MOORE (1779–1852)

Love Is a Mighty Power

Love is a mighty power, a great and complete good.
Love alone lightens every burden, and makes rough places
    smooth.
It bears every hardship as though it were nothing,
And renders all bitterness sweet and acceptable.

Nothing is sweeter than love,
Nothing stronger,
Nothing higher,
Nothing wider,
Nothing more pleasant,
Nothing fuller or better in heaven or earth; for love is born of
    God.

Love flies, runs and leaps for joy.
It is free and unrestrained.
Love knows no limits, but ardently transcends all bounds.
Love feels no burden, takes no account of toil,
Attempts things beyond its strength.

Love sees nothing as impossible,
For it feels able to achieve all things.
It is strange and effective, while those who lack love faint and
    fail.

Love is not fickle and sentimental, nor is it intent on vanities.
Like a living flame and a burning torch, it surges upward and
    surely surmounts every obstacle.

THOMAS À KEMPIS (1379–1471)
From *The Imitation of Christ*

Only Our Love

Only our love hath no decay;
This, no tomorrow hath, nor yesterday,
Running it never runs from us away,
But truly keeps his first, last, everlasting day.

JOHN DONNE (1572–1631)

The First Day

I wish I could remember the first day
First hour, first moment of your meeting me,
If bright or dim the season, it might be
Summer or winter for aught I can say,
So unrecorded did it slip away,
So blind was I to see and to foresee,
So dull to mark the budding of my tree
That would not blossom for many a May.
If only I could recollect it! Such
A day of days! I let it come and go
As traceless as a thaw of bygone snow.
It seemed to mean so little, meant so much!
If only now I could recall that touch,
First touch of hand in hand! – Did one but know!

CHRISTINA ROSSETTI (1830–1894)

Sonnet 116

Let me not to the marriage of true minds
Admit impediments. Love is not love
Which alters when it alteration finds,
Or bends with the remover to remove.
O, no! it is an ever-fixed mark,
That looks on tempests and is never shaken;
It is the star to every wand'ring bark,
Whose worth's unknown, although his height be taken.
Love's not Time's fool, though rosy lips and cheeks
Within his bending sickle's compass come;
Love alters not with his brief hours and weeks,
But bears it out even to the edge of doom.
    If this be error and upon me prov'd,
    I never writ, nor no man ever lov'd.

WILLIAM SHAKESPEARE (1564–1616)

Somewhere

Somewhere there waiteth in this world of ours
For one lone soul, another lonely soul –
Each chasing each through all the weary hours,
And meeting strangely at one sudden goal;
Then blend they – like green leaves with golden flowers,
Into one beautiful and perfect whole –
And life's long night is ended, and the way
Lies open onward to eternal day.

SIR EDWIN ARNOLD (1832–1904)

Sonnet from the Portuguese, XLIII

How do I love thee? Let me count the ways.
I love thee to the depth and breadth and height
My soul can reach, when feeling out of sight
For the ends of Being and ideal Grace.
I love thee to the level of everyday's
Most quiet need, by sun and candlelight.
I love thee freely, as men strive for Right;
I love thee purely, as they turn from Praise.
I love thee with the passion put to use
In my old griefs, and with my childhood's faith.
I love thee with a love I seemed to lose
With my lost saints, – I love thee with the breath,
Smiles, tears, of all my life! – and, if God choose,
I shall but love thee better after death.

ELIZABETH BARRETT BROWNING (1806–1861)

The Bargain

My true love hath my heart, and I have his,
    By just exchange one for another given;
I hold his dear, and mine he cannot miss;
    There never was a better bargain driven:
My true love hath my heart, and I have his.
My heart in me keeps him and me in one;
    My heart in him his thoughts and senses guides;
He loves my heart, for once it was his own;
    I cherish his because in me it bides:
My true love hath my heart, and I have his.

SIR PHILIP SIDNEY (1554–1586)

How Sweet the Moonlight Sleeps

How sweet the moonlight sleeps upon this bank!
Here we will sit and let the sounds of music
Creep in our ears; soft stillness and the night
Become the touches of sweet harmony.
Sit, Jessica. Look how the floor of heaven
Is thick inlaid with patines of bright gold;
There's not the smallest orb which thou behold'st
But in his motion like an angel sings,
Still quiring to the young-eyed cherubins;
Such harmony is in immortal souls,
But whilst this muddy vesture of decay
Doth grossly close it in, we cannot hear it.

WILLIAM SHAKESPEARE (1564–1616)
From *The Merchant of Venice,* Act V, Scene i

The Good-Morrow

I wonder by my troth, what thou and I
Did, till we lov'd? Were we not wean'd till then,
But suck'd on country pleasures, childishly?
Or snorted we in the seven sleepers' den?
'Twas so; but this, all pleasures fancies be.
If ever any beauty I did see,
Which I desir'd, and got, 'twas but a dream of thee.

And now good morrow to our waking souls,
Which watch not one another out of fear;
For love, all love of other sights controls,
And makes one little room, an everywhere.
Let sea-discoverers to new worlds have gone,
Let maps to other, worlds on worlds have shown,
Let us possess one world, each hath one, and is one.

My face in thine eye, thine in mine appears,
And true plain hearts do in the faces rest;
Where can we find two better hemispheres,
Without sharp north, without declining west?
Whatever dies, was not mix'd equally;
If our two loves be one, or, thou and I
Love so alike, that none do slacken, none can die.

JOHN DONNE (1572–1631)

The Passionate Shepherd to His Love

Come live with me and be my Love,
And we will all the pleasures prove,
That hills and valleys, dale and field,
And all the craggy mountains yield.

There will we sit upon the rocks
And see the shepherds feed their flocks,
By shallow rivers, to whose falls
Melodious birds sing madrigals.

There will I make thee beds of roses
And a thousand fragrant posies,
A cap of flowers, and a kirtle
Embroider'd all with leaves of myrtle.

A gown made of the finest wool,
Which from our pretty lambs we pull,
Fair linèd slippers for the cold,
With buckles of the purest gold.

A belt of straw and ivy buds
With coral clasps and amber studs:
And if these pleasures may thee move,
Come live with me and be my Love.

Thy silver dishes for thy meat
As precious as the gods do eat,
Shall on an ivory table be
Prepared each day for thee and me.

The shepherd swains shall dance and sing
For thy delight each May-morning:
If these delights thy mind may move,
Then live with me and be my Love.

CHRISTOPHER MARLOWE (1564–1593)

The Prayer of St Francis

Lord, make me an instrument of your peace.
Where there is hatred, let me sow love.
Where there is injury, pardon.
Where there is doubt, faith.
Where there is despair, hope.
Where there is darkness, light.
Where there is sadness, joy.

O, Divine Master, grant that I may not so much seek
To be consoled, as to console;
To be understood, as to understand;
To be loved as to love;
For it is in giving that we receive,
It is in pardoning that we are pardoned,
And it is in dying that we are born to eternal life.

ST FRANCIS OF ASSISI (1182–1226)

To Anthea, Who May Command Him Anything

Bid me to live, and I will live,
    Thy Protestant to be:
Or bid me love, and I will give
    A loving heart to thee.

A heart as soft, a heart as kind,
    A heart as sound and free
As in the whole world thou canst find,
    That heart I'll give to thee.

Bid that heart stay, and it will stay,
    To honour thy decree:
Or bid it languish quite away,
    And 't shall do so for thee.

Bid me to weep, and I will weep
    While I have eyes to see:
And having none, yet I will keep
    A heart to weep for thee.

Bid me despair, and I'll despair,
    Under that cypress tree:
Or bid me die, and I will dare
    E'en Death, to die for thee.

Thou art my life, my love, my heart,
    The very eyes of me,
And hast command of every part,
    To live and die for thee.

ROBERT HERRICK (1591–1674)

To My Dear Loving Husband

If ever two were one, then surely we.
If ever man were loved by wife, then thee;
If ever wife was happy in a man,
Compare with me, ye woman, if you can.
I prize thy love more than whole mines of gold
Or all the riches that the East doth hold.
My love is such that rivers cannot quench,
Nor ought but love from thee, give recompense.
Thy love is such I can no way repay,
The heavens reward thee manifold, I pray.
The while we live, in love let's so persevere,
That when we live no more, we may live ever.

ANNE BRADSTREET (1612–1672)

PSALMS AND
OLD TESTAMENT READINGS

The Creation

Then God said, 'Let us make humankind in our image, according to our likeness; and let them have dominion over the fish of the sea, and over the birds of the air, and over the cattle, and over all the wild animals of the earth, and over every creeping thing that creeps upon the earth.'

So God created humankind in his image, in the image of God he created them; male and female he created them.

God blessed them, and God said to them, 'Be fruitful and multiply, and fill the earth and subdue it; and have dominion over the fish of the sea and over the birds of the air and over every living thing that moves upon the earth.'

God said, 'See, I have given you every plant yielding seed that is upon the face of all the earth, and every tree with seed in its fruit; you shall have them for food.

'And to every beast of the earth, and to every bird of the air, and to everything that creeps on the earth, everything that has the breath of life, I have given every green plant for food.' And it was so.

God saw everything that he had made, and indeed, it was very good. And there was evening and there was morning, the sixth day.

Thus the heavens and the earth were finished, and all their multitude.

And on the seventh day God finished the work that he had done, and he rested on the seventh day from all the work that he had done.

So God blessed the seventh day and hallowed it, because on it God rested from all the work that he had done in creation.

These are the generations of the heavens and the earth when they were created.

Genesis 1: 26–31; 2: 1–4

God Creates Woman for Man

Then the Lord God said, 'It is not good that the man should be alone; I will make him a helper as his partner.'

So out of the ground the Lord God formed every animal of the field and every bird of the air, and brought them to the man to see what he would call them; and whatever the man called each living creature, that was its name.

The man gave names to all cattle, and to the birds of the air, and to every animal of the field; but for the man there was not found a helper as his partner.

So the Lord God caused a deep sleep to fall upon the man, and he slept; then he took one of his ribs and closed up its place with flesh.

And the rib that the Lord God had taken from the man he made into a woman and brought her to the man.

Then the man said, 'This at last is bone of my bones and flesh of my flesh; this one shall be called woman, for out of Man this one was taken.'

Therefore a man leaves his father and his mother and clings to his wife, and they become one flesh.

GENESIS 2: 18–24

The Constancy of Ruth

But Ruth said, 'Do not press me to leave you or to turn back
from following you! Where you go, I will go; where you
lodge, I will lodge; your people shall be my people, and your
God my God.

'Where you die, I will die – there will I be buried. May the
Lord do thus and so to me, and more as well, if even death
parts me from you!'

Ruth 1: 16–17

O Lord Our Sovereign How Majestic Is Your Name

O Lord, our Sovereign, how majestic is your name in all the earth!
You have set your glory above the heavens.
Out of the mouths of babes and infants you have founded a
    bulwark because of your foes, to silence the enemy and the
    avenger.
When I look at your heavens, the work of your fingers, the
    moon and the stars that you have established; what are
    human beings that you are mindful of them, mortals that
    you care for them?
Yet you have made them a little lower than God, and crowned
    them with glory and honour.
You have given them dominion over the works of your hands;
    you have put all things under their feet, all sheep and oxen,
    and also the beasts of the fields, the birds of the air, and the
    fish of the sea, whatever passes along the paths of the seas.
O Lord, our Sovereign, how majestic is your name in all the earth!

Psalm 8

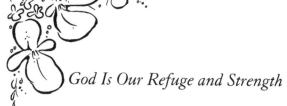 *God Is Our Refuge and Strength*

God is our refuge and strength, a very present help in trouble.

Therefore we will not fear, though the earth should change,
   though the mountains shake in the heart of the sea; though
   its waters roar and foam, though the mountains tremble
   with its tumult.

There is a river whose streams make glad the city of God, the
   holy habitation of the Most High.

God is in the midst of the city; it shall not be moved; God will
   help it when the morning dawns.

The nations are in an uproar, the kingdoms totter; he utters
   his voice, the earth melts.

The Lord of hosts is with us; the God of Jacob is our refuge.

Come, behold the works of the Lord; see what desolations he
   has brought on the earth.

He makes wars cease to the end of the earth; he breaks the
   bow, and shatters the spear; he burns the shields with fire.

'Be still, and know that I am God! I am exalted among the
   nations, I am exalted in the earth.'

The Lord of hosts is with us; the God of Jacob is our refuge.

PSALM 46

May God Be Gracious to Us and Bless Us

May God be gracious to us and bless us and make his face to
shine upon us, that your way may be known upon earth,
your saving power among all nations.
Let the peoples praise you, O God; let all the peoples praise you.
Let the nations be glad and sing for joy, for you judge the
peoples with equity and guide the nations upon earth.
Let the peoples praise you, O God; let all the peoples praise you.
The earth has yielded its increase; God, our God, has blessed us.
May God continue to bless us; let all the ends of the earth
revere him.

PSALM 67

Make a Joyful Noise to the Lord

Make a joyful noise to the Lord, all the earth.
Worship the Lord with gladness; come into his presence with
singing.
Know that the Lord is God. It is he that made us, and we are
his; we are his people, and the sheep of his pasture.
Enter his gates with thanksgiving, and his courts with praise.
Give thanks to him, bless his name.
For the Lord is good; his steadfast love endures for ever, and
his faithfulness to all generations.

PSALM 100

I Lift Up My Eyes to the Hills

I lift up my eyes to the hills – from where will my help come?
My help comes from the Lord, who made heaven and earth.
He will not let your foot be moved; he who keeps you will not
    slumber.
He who keeps Israel will neither slumber nor sleep.
The Lord is your keeper; the Lord is your shade at your right
    hand.
The sun shall not strike you by day, nor the moon by night.
The Lord will keep you from all evil; he will keep your life.
The Lord will keep your going out and your coming in from
    this time on and forever more.

PSALM 121

Unless the Lord Builds the House

Unless the Lord builds the house, those who build it labour in
    vain.
Unless the Lord guards the city, the guard keeps watch in vain.
It is in vain that you rise up early and go late to rest, eating the
    bread of anxious toil; for he gives sleep to his beloved.
Sons are indeed a heritage from the Lord, the fruit of the
    womb a reward.
Like arrows in the hand of a warrior are the sons of one's youth.
Happy is the man who has his quiver full of them.
He shall not be put to shame when he speaks with his enemies
    in the gate.

PSALM 127

Happy Is Everyone Who Fears the Lord

Happy is everyone who fears the Lord, who walks in his ways.
You shall eat the fruit of the labour of your hands; you shall be
    happy, and it shall go well with you.
Your wife will be like a fruitful vine within your house; your
    children will be like olive shoots around your table.
Thus shall the man be blessed who fears the Lord.
The Lord bless you from Zion. May you see the prosperity of
    Jerusalem all the days of your life.
May you see your children's children.
Peace be upon Israel!

PSALM 128

I Give You Thanks, O Lord

I give you thanks, O Lord, with my whole heart; before the
    gods I sing your praise;
I bow down towards your holy temple and give thanks to your
    name for your steadfast love and your faithfulness; for you
    have exalted your name and your word above everything.
On the day I called, you answered me, you increased my
    strength of soul.
All the kings of the earth shall praise you, O Lord, for they
    have heard the words of your mouth.
They shall sing of the ways of the Lord, for great is the glory
    of the Lord.
For though the Lord is high, he regards the lowly; but the
    haughty he perceives from far away.
Though I walk in the midst of trouble, you preserve me
    against the wrath of my enemies; you stretch out your
    hand, and your right hand delivers me.
The Lord will fulfil his purpose for me; your steadfast love,
    O Lord, endures for ever.
Do not forsake the work of your hands.

PSALM 138

Praise the Lord!

Praise the Lord!
Praise God in his sanctuary; praise him in his mighty
    firmament!
Praise him for his mighty deeds; praise him according to his
    surpassing greatness!
Praise him with trumpet sound; praise him with lute and
    harp!
Praise him with tambourine and dance; praise him with
    strings and pipe!
Praise him with clanging cymbals; praise him with loud
    clashing cymbals!
Let everything that breathes praise the Lord!
Praise the Lord!

PSALM 150

Remember the Teaching of the Scriptures

My child, do not forget my teaching, but let your heart keep my commandments; for length of days and years of life and abundant welfare they will give you.

Do not let loyalty and faithfulness forsake you; bind them round your neck, write them on the tablet of your heart.

So you will find favour and good repute in the sight of God and of people.

Trust in the Lord with all your heart, and do not rely on your own insight.

In all your ways acknowledge him, and he will make straight your paths.

Happy are those who find wisdom, and those who get understanding, for her income is better than silver, and her revenue better than gold.

She is more precious than jewels, and nothing you desire can compare with her.

Long life is in her right hand; in her left hand are riches and honour.

Her ways are ways of pleasantness, and all her paths are peace.

She is a tree of life to those who lay hold of her; those who hold her fast are called happy.

The Lord by wisdom founded the earth; by understanding he established the heavens; by his knowledge the deeps broke open, and the clouds drop down the dew.

My child, do not let these escape from your sight: keep sound wisdom and prudence, and they will be life for your soul and adornment for your neck.

Then you will walk on your way securely and your foot will not stumble.

If you sit down, you will not be afraid; when you lie down, your sleep will be sweet.

PROVERBS 3: 1–6, 13–24

Two Are Better than One

Two are better than one, because they have a good reward for their toil.

For if they fall, one will lift up the other; but woe to one who is alone and falls and does not have another to help.

Again, if two lie together, they keep warm; but how can one keep warm alone?

And though one might prevail against another, two will withstand one. A threefold cord is not quickly broken.

ECCLESIASTES 4: 9–12

Love Is as Strong as Death

Set me as a seal upon your heart, as a seal upon your arm; for love is strong as death, passion fierce as the grave. Its flashes are flashes of fire, a raging flame.

Many waters cannot quench love, neither can floods drown it. If one offered for love all the wealth of one's house, it would be utterly scorned.

THE SONG OF SOLOMON 8: 6–7

The Qualities of a Good Wife

A capable wife who can find? She is far more precious than jewels.

The heart of her husband trusts in her, and he will have no lack of gain.

She does him good, and not harm, all the days of her life.

She seeks wool and flax, and works with willing hands.

She is like the ships of the merchant, she brings her food from far away.

She rises while it is still night and provides food for her household and tasks for her servant-girls.

She considers a field and buys it: with the fruit of her hands she plants a vineyard.

She girds herself with strength and makes her arms strong.

She perceives that her merchandise is profitable.

Her lamp does not go out at night.

She puts her hands to the distaff, and her hands hold the spindle.

She opens her hand to the poor, and reaches out her hands to the needy.

She is not afraid for her household when it snows, for her household are clothed in crimson.

She makes herself coverings; her clothing is fine linen and purple.

Her husband is known in the city gates, taking his seat among the elders of the land.

She makes linen garments and sells them; she supplies the merchant with sashes.

Strength and dignity are her clothing, and she laughs at the time to come.

She opens her mouth with wisdom, and the teaching of kindness is on her tongue.

She looks well to the ways of her household, and does not eat the bread of idleness.

Her children rise up and call her happy; her husband too, and he praises her: 'Many women have done excellently, but you surpass them all.'

Charm is deceitful, and beauty is vain, but a woman who fears the Lord is to be praised.

Give her a share in the fruit of her hands, and let her works praise her in the city gates.

PROVERBS 31: 10–31

Rejoice in the Lord

I will greatly rejoice in the Lord, my whole being shall exult in my God; for he has clothed me with the garments of salvation, he has covered me with the robe of righteousness, as a bridegroom decks himself with a garland, and as a bride adorns herself with her jewels.

For as the earth brings forth its shoots and as a garden causes what is sown in it to spring up, so the Lord God will cause righteousness and praise to spring up before all the nations.

ISAIAH 61: 10–11

NEW TESTAMENT READINGS

The Beatitudes

When Jesus saw the crowds, he went up the mountain; and after he sat down, his disciples came to him.

Then he began to speak, and taught them, saying:

'Blessed are the poor in spirit, for theirs is the kingdom of heaven.

'Blessed are those who mourn, for they will be comforted.

'Blessed are the meek, for they will inherit the earth.

'Blessed are those who hunger and thirst for righteousness, for they will be filled.

'Blessed are the merciful, for they will receive mercy.

'Blessed are the pure in heart, for they will see God.

'Blessed are the peacemakers, for they will be called children of God.

'Blessed are those who are persecuted for righteousness' sake, for theirs is the kingdom of heaven.

'Blessed are you when people revile you and persecute you and utter all kinds of evil against you falsely on my account.

'Rejoice and be glad, for your reward is great in heaven, for in the same way they persecuted the prophets who were before you.'

MATTHEW 5: 1–12

Build Your House on a Rock

'Not everyone who says to me, "Lord, Lord," will enter the kingdom of heaven, but only one who does the will of my Father in heaven.

'On that day many will say to me, "Lord, Lord, did we not prophesy in your name, and cast out demons in your name, and do many deeds of power in your name?"

'Then I will declare to them, "I never knew you; go away from me, you evildoers."

'Everyone then who hears these words of mine and acts on them will be like a wise man who built his house on rock.

'The rain fell, the floods came, and the winds blew and beat on that house, but it did not fall, because it had been founded on rock.

'And everyone who hears these words of mine and does not act on them will be like a foolish man who built his house on sand.

'The rain fell, and the floods came, and the winds blew and beat against that house, and it fell – and great was its fall!'

Now when Jesus had finished saying these things, the crowds were astounded at his teaching, for he taught them as one having authority, and not as their scribes.

MATTHEW 7: 21–29

The Two Great Commandments

One of the scribes came near and heard them disputing with one another, and seeing that he answered them well, he asked him, 'Which commandment is the first of all?'

Jesus answered, 'The first is, "Hear, O Israel; the Lord our God the Lord is one; you shall love the Lord your God with all your heart, and with all your soul, and with all your mind, and with all your strength."

'The second is this, "You shall love your neighbour as yourself." There is no other commandment greater than these.'

Then the scribe said to him, 'You are right, Teacher ... this is much more important than all whole burnt offerings and sacrifices.'

When Jesus saw that he answered wisely, he said to him, 'You are not far from the kingdom of God.' After that no one dared to ask him any question.

MARK 12: 28–34

Reflecting God's Love

As the Father has loved me, so I have loved you; abide in my love.

If you keep my commandments, you will abide in my love, just as I have kept my Father's commandments and abide in his love.

I have said these things to you so that my joy may be in you, and that your joy may be complete.

This is my commandment, that you love one another as I have loved you.

JOHN 15: 9–12

Let Love Be Genuine

Let love be genuine; hate what is evil, hold fast to what is good;

Love one another with mutual affection; outdo one another in showing honour.

Do not lag in zeal, be ardent in spirit, serve the Lord.

Rejoice in hope, be patient in suffering, persevere in prayer.

Contribute to the needs of the saints; extend hospitality to strangers.

Bless those who persecute you; bless and do not curse them.

Rejoice with those who rejoice, weep with those who weep.

Live in harmony with one another; do not be haughty, but associate with the lowly; do not claim to be wiser than you are.

Do not repay anyone evil for evil, but take thought for what is noble in the sight of all.

If it is possible, so far as it depends on you, live peaceably with all.

ROMANS 12: 9–18

St Paul's Hymn of Love

But strive for the greater gifts. And I will show you a still more excellent way.

If I speak in the tongues of mortals and of angels, but do not have love, I am a noisy gong or a clanging cymbal.

And if I have prophetic powers, and understand all mysteries and all knowledge, and if I have all faith, so as to remove mountains, but do not have love, I am nothing.

If I give away all my possessions, and if I hand over my body so that I may boast, but do not have love, I gain nothing.

Love is patient; love is kind; love is not envious or boastful or arrogant or rude.

It does not insist on its own way; it is not irritable or resentful; it does not rejoice in wrongdoing, but rejoices in the truth.

It bears all things, believes all things, hopes all things, endures all things.

Love never ends. But as for prophecies, they will come to an end; as for tongues, they will cease; as for knowledge, it will come to an end.

For we know only in part, and we prophesy only in part; but when the complete comes, the partial will come to an end.

When I was a child, I spoke like a child, I thought like a child, I reasoned like a child; when I became an adult, I put an end to childish ways.

For now we see in a mirror, dimly, but then we will see face to face. Now I know only in part; then I will know fully, even as I have been fully known.

And now faith, hope, and love abide, these three; and the greatest of these is love.

1 CORINTHIANS 12: 31; 13: 1–13

Be Strengthened by God's Love

For this reason I bow my knees before the Father, from whom every family in heaven and on earth takes its name.

I pray that, according to the riches of his glory, he may grant that you may be strengthened in your inner being with power through his Spirit, and that Christ may dwell in your hearts through faith, as you are being rooted and grounded in love.

I pray that you may have the power to comprehend, with all the saints, what is the breadth and length and height and depth, and to know the love of Christ that surpasses knowledge, so that you may be filled with all the fullness of God.

EPHESIANS 3: 14–19

Clothe Yourselves with Love

As God's chosen ones, holy and beloved, clothe yourselves with compassion, kindness, humility, meekness, and patience.

Bear with one another and, if anyone has a complaint against another, forgive each other; just as the Lord has forgiven you, so you also must forgive.

Above all, clothe yourselves with love, which binds everything together in perfect harmony.

And let the peace of Christ rule in your hearts, to which indeed you were called in the one body. And be thankful.

Let the word of Christ dwell in you richly; teach and admonish one another in all wisdom; and with gratitude in your hearts sing psalms, hymns, and spiritual songs to God.

And whatever you do, in word or deed, do everything in the name of the Lord Jesus, giving thanks to God the Father through him.

COLOSSIANS 3: 12–17

Show Love in What You Do

Little children, let us love, not in word or speech, but in truth and action.

And by this we will know that we are from the truth and will reassure our hearts before him whenever our hearts condemn us; for God is greater than our hearts, and he knows everything.

Beloved, if our hearts do not condemn us, we have boldness before God; and we receive from him whatever we ask, because we obey his commandments and do what pleases him.

And this is his commandment, that we should believe in the name of his Son Jesus Christ and love one another, just as he has commanded us.

All who obey his commandments abide in him, and he abides in them. And by this we know that he abides in us, by the Spirit that he has given us.

1 JOHN 3: 18–24

God Is Love

Beloved, let us love one another, because love is from God; everyone who loves is born of God and knows God.

Whoever does not love does not know God, for God is love.

God's love was revealed among us in this way: God sent his only Son into the world so that we might love through him.

In this is love, not that we loved God but that he loved us and sent his Son to be the atoning sacrifice for our sins.

Beloved, since God loved us so much, we also ought to love one another.

No one has ever seen God; if we love one another, God lives in us, and his love is perfected in us.

By this we know that we abide in him and he in us, because he has given us of his Spirit.

And we have seen and do testify that the Father has sent his Son as the Saviour of the world.

God abides in those who confess that Jesus is the Son of God, and they abide in God. So we have known and believe the love that God has for us.

God is love, and those who abide in love abide in God, and God abides in them.

1 JOHN 4: 7–16

MUSICAL IDEAS

Choosing Your Music

The music you choose for your wedding plays a crucial part in setting the style of the ceremony and so it is important to spend time finding pieces that will create the kind of atmosphere you want. There are, of course, some pieces of music that immediately spring to mind when weddings are mentioned: Mendelssohn's 'Wedding March', for example, never seems to go out of fashion. But perhaps you want something a little different, more tailored to your individual style. You may already have a number of favourite pieces in mind or be looking for helpful suggestions and guidance. In any event you must discuss your selection with either the minister or the Superintendent Registrar.

The principal opportunities for music at church and civil ceremonies are much the same. You will need to choose music for four occasions during the ceremony:

- Music to be played before the service or ceremony (prelude music)
- Music to accompany the entrance of the bridal party (processional music)
- Music to be played during the signing of the register
- Music for the exit of the bridal couple at the end of the ceremony (recessional music).

In addition, for a church wedding, you will need to choose two or three hymns.

Religious Ceremonies

You will find that both the minister and the church organist will be happy to help and advise you on the choice of hymns and music.

Hymns

Most church wedding services include two or three hymns and you are free to choose any that are appropriate. There are many suitable hymns based on Christian themes of love, prayer and praise. One way of achieving a good balance could be to choose one about love at the beginning (where the words of the service are all about love), then a prayerful hymn or psalm in the middle (to reflect the prayers that are said for the marriage), and then a hymn of praise and celebration at the end.

It is a good idea to look through the hymn books that the church uses and ask the organist to play the tunes for you. Some hymns may be sung to more than one tune and you will want to make sure that you have the ones that you like – and that the congregation will know well. It may also be that you have a hymn tune in mind but need to find a hymn with appropriate words to go with it. The organist or minister can help with both these issues, or you can check the index to the music editions of the hymn book. Long hymns can have a verse or two omitted if wished and any verses that are inappropriate for a wedding can also be left out. Again the minister and organist can advise.

It may be a good idea to have the church choir attend the service. A choir can help to lead the congregational singing and perform any choral music that you may have chosen as part of the service. Alternatively, you could employ four to six experienced choral singers to be your choir for the occasion.

Choirs and vocal soloists are the most common providers of music at wedding services but other possibilities could include musical ensembles playing any kind of instrument, including guitar, trumpet, harp, strings and wind.

It is most important to discuss all the music with the organist and choirmaster to ensure that they are comfortable and familiar with the items you have chosen. This is also true of any soloist or ensemble – vocal or instrumental – you may wish to engage.

Civil Ceremonies

Without music, a civil ceremony is very short. Music, like readings of poetry or prose, offers a means of enhancing your wedding vows and giving more time and substance to your ceremony.

By law, only non-religious music and readings are allowed at civil ceremonies. The 'non-religious' definition usually means that the music does not contain words such as 'Lord', 'God', 'Heaven' or 'Jesus', and it should not detract from the solemnity of the occasion. This ruling is subject to the interpretation of individual superintendent registrars and so you should submit your music list for approval before the ceremony. Most registrars are more than happy to advise you and many district authorities produce a list of suggestions to help you make your choice.

Civil ceremonies may take place at either a register office or licensed premises, where you can also have the reception. Both venues will usually have a sound system for playing pre-recorded music or you may supply your own. Register offices usually also have a selection of CDs from which you can choose music although the size of the selection may vary. If you will be relying on a CD or cassette player, rather than an organist or other live musicians, it is best to record all your chosen music on to a special CD or tape. Switching from one to another can cause confusion, and finding the right track in a compilation may take time and interrupt the flow of events. You will also be able to keep the recording as a memento of the day.

If you wish to have 'live' music, it may be possible to bring in an electronic keyboard for piano/organ music or to accompany a soloist, or you may wish to engage musicians, such as a solo guitarist, string quartet or other ensemble. Again it is wise to discuss this in advance with the Superintendent Registrar. It goes without saying that you should always be sure of the standard of any performers you engage!

Do check the size of the venue as this can have a bearing on your choice of musicians. Register offices are often quite cramped, although licensed venues are usually much larger, making it easier to accommodate soloists or other performers who may then stay on to provide musical entertainment at the reception.

Register office ceremonies may also be subject to time constraints, as several ceremonies may be being held in succession on the same day. Ceremonies at licensed premises are likely to be more leisurely, giving greater freedom in deciding the number of pieces you would like played.

On the following pages you will find a wide variety of suitable music, ranging from classical to pop. In choosing, it is important to think carefully about the atmosphere you are trying to create – whatever your choice of style of ceremony, the music should complement it. It is worth remembering that traditional doesn't have to mean classical and secular doesn't have to mean pop.

There are a number of very helpful websites on the internet, where you can find lists of suitable pieces of music and through which you can purchase wedding music CDs.

Whatever the style of your ceremony, think about what will be happening at each stage and try to match the music to the mood of the moment. To give cohesion to the ceremony, you may like to choose musical items that are linked by a common theme. For example, you might choose a selection of contemporary love songs or five baroque pieces by different composers. For this reason, compilation CDs – both classical and contemporary – are particularly useful when it comes to putting together the right selection of music. We have not included any as they are changed and deleted so frequently, but you will find a huge selection in any high street music dealer. The traditional classical music listed may suit your choice or there is a wide variety of other music styles to choose from e.g. operatic arias, classical songs (in different languages), classic music theatre songs, romantic songs.

We have not listed alternative secular music as the scope is immense and very much a matter of personal choice.

Before the Service and
During the Signing of the Register

At both these times, there will be some movement and conversation amongst the guests, so you require music that is not too intrusive. Remember that you want an atmosphere that is calm but not funereal!

Bach	Air on a G String
Bach	Jesu, Joy of Man's Desiring
Bach	Sheep May Safely Graze
Bach/Gounod	Ave Maria
Dvořák	Theme from the 'New World' Symphony
Elgar	Chanson de Matin
Elgar	Nimrod
Elgar	Salut d'Amour
Fauré	Aprés un rêve
Fauré	Berceuse (Dolly Suite)
Fauré	Pavane
Handel	Alla Siciliano from 'Music for the Royal Fireworks'
Handel	Hornpipe from 'The Water Music'
Handel	Minuet (Berenice)
Handel	Organ Concerto in F
Handel	Serse from 'Xerxes'
Haydn	Trumpet Concerto (Slow Movement)
Haydn	St Anthony Chorale
Pachelbel	Canon in D
Satie	Gymnopedie
Walton	Popular Song (Façade)
Warlock	Capriol Suite

Wesley	Air and Gavotte
Wesley	Air and Gavotte in F
Vaughan Williams	Greensleeves

Instead of instrumental music, you may prefer to have choral works and modern songs sung by a soloist or choir.
For example:

Bach/Gounod	Ave Maria
Fauré	Cantique de Jean Racine
Franck	Panis Angelicus
Traditional Irish	I Would Be True
Rutter	A Gaelic Blessing
Schubert	Ave Maria
Walford Davies	God Be in My Head
Bernstein	One Hand, One Heart *(West Side Story)*
Horner/Jennings	My Heart Will Go On *(Titanic)*
Lloyd-Webber	Love Changes Everything *(Aspects of Love)*

To Accompany the Entrance of the Bridal Party

This music should be designed to catch the attention of the guests and announce that the ceremony is about to begin. The pace may vary from stately to something more sprightly, but it should be suitable to accompany the bride or couple as they walk in. (It is worth practising beforehand to make sure that you are comfortable with it.)

Note: Some of these are also suitable for use at the end of the service/ceremony.

Bach	Allegro from 'Brandenburg Concerto'
Bliss	Wedding Fanfare
Boyce	A Trumpet Voluntary
Clarke	Trumpet Voluntary
Handel	Arrival of the Queen of Sheba
Handel	Hornpipe in D from 'The Water Music'
Handel	March form Judas Maccabaeus
Handel	March from Scipio
Handel	Music for the Royal Fireworks
Hollins	Trumpet Minuet
Ireland	Alla Marcia
Purcell	Trumpet Tune in D
Saint-Saens	Third Organ Symphony (4th Movement)
Saint-Saens	Benediction Nuptiale
Verdi	Grand March from 'Aida'
Vivaldi	Spring from 'The Four Seasons'
Wagner	Bridal March from 'Lohengrin'

To Accompany the Exit of the Bride and Groom

Once again, the emphasis is on the joyful, celebratory aspects of the occasion. Like the music for the entrance, the tone should be bright and cheerful.

Bach	Fugue in D – BWV 532
Bach	Prelude in G – BWV 541
Bach	Toccata in C – BWV564
Bach	Toccata and Fugue in D minor – BWV 565
Clarke	Trumpet Voluntary Op. 6 No. 5
Elgar	Pomp and Circumstance March No. 4
Handel	Hallelujah Chorus from 'The Messiah'
Handel	Hornpipe from 'The Water Music'
Karg-Elert	Nun Dankert Alle Gott
Lefebvre-Wely	Sortie E flat and B flat
Mendelssohn	The Wedding March
Mozart	Overture from 'The Marriage of Figaro'
Purcell	Trumpet Tune and Air in C
Stanley	Trumpet Voluntary Op. 6. No. 5
Strauss	Radetsky March
Vierne	Finale from Symphony No.1
Walton	Crown Imperial
Wesley	Choral Song
Widor	Marche Pontificale from Symphony No.1
Widor	Toccata from the Fifth Symphony

Hymns

Since nothing of a religious nature can be included in a civil ceremony, hymns may only be sung at a church wedding. When making your selection, think about the sort of message you want to convey – hymns of love, praise and thanks are, in general, most appropriate. Remember that many hymns may be sung to several different tunes and check that the organist plays one that is well known to everyone.

The suggestions here have been selected from *Hymns Ancient and Modern (New Standard)* and *Mission Praise,* both of which are available from good bookshops in both hardback and paperback editions, and also in editions containing both words and music.

All my hope on God is founded
All creatures of our God and king
All things bright and beautiful
All people that on earth do dwell
And did those feet in ancient time (Jerusalem)
Angel voices ever singing
Amazing grace
At the name of Jesus
Be thou my vision, O Lord of my heart
Bind us together Lord
Breathe on me, breath of God
Christ is made the sure foundation
Come down, O love divine
Crown him with many crowns
Dear Lord and father of mankind
Father, hear the prayer we offer
Fill thou my life, O Lord my God

For the beauty of the earth
Forth in thy name, O Lord, I go
Give me joy in my heart
God is love, his the care
God of mercy, God of grace
Gracious Spirit, Holy Ghost
Guide me, O thou great redeemer
He's got the whole world in his hands
Help us to help each other Lord
Immortal, invisible God only wise
I danced in the morning (Lord of the Dance)
I vow to thee, my country
In heavenly love abiding
Jesus, good above all other
King of glory, king of peace
Lead us, heavenly father, lead us
Lift up your hearts, we lift them Lord to thee
Lord for the years
Lord of all hopefulness, Lord of all joy
Lord of all power
Lord Jesus Christ
Love divine, all loves excelling
Make me a channel of your peace
Morning has broken
Now thank we all our God
O God, whose loving hand has led
O Holy Spirit, Lord of grace
O Jesus, I have promised
O perfect love, all human thoughts transcending
O praise ye the Lord
O thou who camest from above
O worship the king, all glorious above

Peace is flowing like a river
Praise my soul the King of Heaven
Praise the Lord! Ye heavens adore him
Praise to the Lord, the Almighty
Rejoice, the Lord is king
Seek ye first the kingdom of God
Take my life and let it be
Tell out my soul the greatness of the Lord
The king of love my shepherd is
The Lord's my shepherd
The Spirit lives to set us free
Thine for ever! God of love
Through all the changing scenes
What a friend we have in Jesus
Ye holy angels bright

Useful websites

The Wedding Music Company
This is a commercial, but very helpful, organisation whose web pages contain extremely useful information, from CDs of wedding music to helping you to find a professional choir or musicians. Visit www.weddingmusic.co.uk.

Other sites
You can also find information at:
www.weddingguide.co.uk
www.webwedding.co.uk
www.weddingsongs.co.uk

Acknowledgements

'Blessing for a marriage' by James Dillet Freeman. Reprinted by permission of The Unity School of Christianity, Unity Village, Missouri 64065, USA.

Extract from *Gift from the Sea* by Anne Morrow Lindbergh. Reprinted by permission of Pantheon Books, a division of Random House Inc. © 1955, 1975, renewed 1983 by Anne Morrow Lindbergh.

'A third body' by Robert Bly from *Loving a Woman in Two Worlds*. © 1985 Robert Bly. Reprinted by permission of Doubleday, a division of Bantam Doubleday Dell Publishing Group Inc.

'He wishes for the cloths of heaven' and 'When you are old' by W.B. Yeats. © A.P. Wyatt. Reprinted from *The Collected Poems of W.B. Yeats* by permission of A.P. Wyatt on behalf of Michael B. Yeats.

'Looking for your face' from *The Love Poems of Rumi,* translated by Fereydoun Kia, edited by Deepak Chopra, published by Rider. © 1998 Deepak Chopra. Reprinted by permission of The Random House Group Ltd.

'Deep in my heart' by Michael Forster. © Kevin Mayhew Ltd, Buxhall, Stowmarket, Suffolk IP14 3BW. Used by permission from *A Book of Married Love*.

'Seasons come, seasons go' by Michael Cockett. © Kevin Mayhew Ltd, Buxhall, Stowmarket, Suffolk IP14 3BW. Used by permission from *Hymns Old and New*.

'I do, I will, I have' by Ogden Nash from *Marriage Lines – Notes of a Student Husband*. © 1949 by Ogden Nash. Reprinted by permission of Curtis Brown Ltd.

'Reprise' by Ogden Nash. © 1949 by Ogden Nash. Reprinted by permission of Curtis Brown Ltd.

'Love (is the river of life)' by Henry Ward Beecher and 'The heart's anchor' by William Winter. Reprinted from *Romance* with permission by Barbour Publishing Inc.

'i carry your heart with me(i carry it in)' E.E. Cummings, edited by George J. Firmage, by permission of W.W. Norton & Co. Ltd. © 1991 by the Trustees for the E.E. Cummings Trust and George James Firmage.

'The confirmation' by E. Muir from *Collected Poems*. Reprinted by permission of Faber and Faber Ltd.

'Oh tell me the truth about love', by W.H. Auden.

'What is love?' by Sherree Louise Hamblyn from *A Way with Words*, published by Poetry Now. Reprinted by permission of the author.

'The song of love' by Rainer Maria Rilke from *Thirty-one Poems by Rainer Maria Rilke*. © Ludwig Lewisohn. Reprinted with permission of Beechhurst Press, Bernard Ackerman Inc., 116 East 19th Street, New York, USA.

'Now touch the air softly' from 'A pavane for the nursery' by William Jay Smith from *The World Beneath the Window: Poems 1937–1997*. © 1998 (Copyright Holder). Reprinted by permission of The John Hopkins University Press.

'Yes I'll marry you dear' by Pam Ayres from *The Works*. Reprinted by permission of BBC Worldwide Ltd.

'The path of marriage', extract from 'Poetry on marriage' by Wendell Berry, from *Standing by Words*. © Wendell Berry. Reprinted by permission of Wendell Berry.

'The demands of love' from *Letters to a Young Poet* by Rainer Maria Rilke. © Stephen Mitchell. Reprinted by permission of Random House Inc.

Extracts from 'The Imitation of Christ' by Thomas à Kempis, translated by Stephen Mitchell, and 'The tao of marriage' by Stephen Mitchell from *Into the Garden: A Wedding Anthology*, edited Robert Hass and Stephen Mitchell. © 1993 Robert Hass and Stephen Mitchell. Reprinted by permission of HarperCollins Publishers Inc.

'A dedication to my wife' by T.S. Eliot from *Collected Poems, 1909–1962*. © 1936 by Harcourt Inc. copyright © 1964, 1963 by T.S. Eliot. Reprinted by permission of Faber and Faber Ltd.

'Marriage: the beginning of an enterprise' by Pam Brown, extract from *Happy Anniversary*. © Helen Exley 1991, 2002. Used by permission of Exley Publications Ltd.

'A creed to live by' by Nancye Sims. © 2002 Blue Mountain Arts. Reprinted by permission of the author.

Index